Henslew

Eddie Mair is the presenter of BBC Radio 4's *PM* and co-presents *iPM*. He has won seven gold Radio Academy awards. He also writes for *Radio Times*, and has won no awards for that.

A Good Face for Radio

Confessions of a Radio Head

EDDIE MAIR

ABACUS

First published in Great Britain in 2017 by Little, Brown
This paperback edition published in 2018 by Abacus

1 3 5 7 9 10 8 6 4 2

A CIP catalogue record for this book
is available from the British Library.

ISBN 978-0-349-14315-6

Typeset in Bembo by M Rules
Printed and bound in Great Britain by
Clays Ltd, Elcograf S.p.A.

Papers used by Abacus are from well-managed forests
and other responsible sources.

MIX
Paper from
responsible sources
FSC® C104740

Abacus
An imprint of
Little, Brown Book Group
Carmelite House
50 Victoria Embankment
London EC4Y 0DZ

An Hachette UK Company
www.hachette.co.uk

www.littlebrown.co.uk

INTRODUCTION

I've never kept a diary.

I've never kept a llama either, yet I present this book to you as a diary rather than a domesticated South American camelid.

Since 2010 I've been recording my life and reflections in the pages of *Radio Times*. You'll find me there every week, nestling between the back end of the TV listings and the front end of the radio listings. It's dry and reasonably comfortable. Most readers never notice me, as I huddle there against the cold. They hurry past, rarely looking me in the eye, en route to reading the letters griping about mumbling on telly, and the special offers on leather-bound *Radio Times* holders.

The column began as a way of repaying a poker debt to the magazine's editor. He has no tell, you know. David Attenborough's in so deep he has to keep filming penguins mating. He's ninety-one.

I imagined the column would last only a few weeks, like a Nigel Farage resignation or a Trump policy position. But weeks became months and months became years. Well, you're familiar with the Gregorian calendar.

Recently I was thumbing through my back issues (still

an offence in Oklahoma) when it occurred to me that these columns were, in effect, my diaries. Sometimes searingly personal: you'll wince when I relay the full horror of realising that I, Eddie Mair, might have to wear specs. On other occasions, the diaries chronicle the significant news events of our time: you'll find on these pages the inside story of some of our country's darkest hours, when Robert Peston left the BBC under a considerable cloud. But mainly the diaries are a masterclass in whining about the BBC and some of the people I am forced to work with.

Martha Kearney and her swarm of bees. Corrie Corfield, often found prostrate in Broadcasting House reception. Susan Rae and her moist brownies. You'll read too of what it's like to pretend to be Andrew Marr, Jeremy Paxman and Jonathan Dimbleby. The underwear for one of them will shock you.

In preparing these diaries I've been inspired by those great diarists, Alan Clark, Samuel Pepys and Letts. It would be absurd to make overblown claims about these diaries but it's likely that historians will use this book as the definitive account of the years 2010 to 2017: the main part of that decade between the noughties and the twenties for which no one has really nailed a name. Therefore you are reading the first draft of history, and I really mean that. As you'll become aware, I never rewrite.

To any colleagues who may be offended by inclusion in these diaries, I say this: have a word with everyone else who's horrified at *not* being included (you know who you are, Tony).

To my colleagues who may be offended by what I've written in this introduction, I say: Corrie, I have the photographs and we both know it.

To anyone who thinks my handsome features on the cover are at odds with the title of the book, I refer you to my remarks about needing specs. I do indeed have a face for radio, along with fingers for playing the piano badly and a bald patch for screening movies in Cinemascope. Self-acceptance is the route to richness. As it happens that's the title of my next book, which turns the accepted norms of self-help and moves into an unexplored area: helping yourself to other people's things.

For now though, I give you my life, in these pages, with love, respect and – as colleagues will tell you – a little too much aftershave.

2010

How I made Bono cry

And it wasn't deliberate – I just asked about Pavarotti

One of this week's big cinema releases is *Death at a Funeral*. I wouldn't normally stray into Barry Norman's territory, though do watch out for my forthcoming 'Eddie Mair's Zesty Enchilada Season and Sauce' next to the toilet paper at your local supermarket. I haven't seen the film but watching a trailer for it at the cinema recently made me sit up – and not just because, like all trailers, it was playing out at a million decibels.

'I've seen this film before,' I said, and was shushed by the woman behind me. 'I've seen this film before,' I said to myself. It all looked very familiar but somehow strange – like watching the first Prime Minister's Questions of the new term last week. On arriving home, extensive research (thank you internet!) revealed that this week's film starring Chris Rock is indeed a remake of the 2007 British film of the same name, which I watched recently on DVD. They're both black comedies but the first one starred white people.

Making death a laughing matter is a serious business. I'm strangely drawn to a website called Death List. At the beginning of every year it draws up a list of fifty celebrities it thinks might die before 31 December. In the event that someone passes away, they are crossed off the list. It's been going for years. Clive Dunn has been on every one. At the time of writing, it has not been a bumper year for them. It's June, and J. D. Salinger and Michael Foot were the only names on the Death List to have died until Dennis Hopper succumbed at the end of May. Last year they managed twelve.

A sick list? Perhaps. But newspapers are always preparing for celebrity deaths – just less publicly than the Death List's brazen approach. Every day obituary writers will contact people to ask for a comment about someone who's still very much alive, so that when they do die the newspaper has something ready. Radio also prepares for celebrity deaths, though this doesn't usually involve phoning friends. The time is used properly to collate archive sound clips: a politician's moments of triumph and defeat; a pop star's greatest hits, as well as their battles with substance abuse.

This means that when we get news of a celebrity death it falls to a producer to telephone unsuspecting friends to tell them about it and ask if they would come on the radio to say a few words. People in the business of show understand how this works and often kindly agree to appear despite their grief. The instant eulogy. Some people are very good at it. One actor I know began to dread the phone ringing because it was usually the BBC telling her that another thespian had died. On the other hand, a colleague once telephoned a well-known sports star and broke the news that a good friend of hers – a famous commentator – had died. The sports star was asked if, in her grief, she'd be able to say a few words on the programme, and she said she would, in return for fifty quid.

I hate doing those interviews. I made Bono cry (talking

about Pavarotti). Last week, during an interview with Tracy Emin about Louise Bourgeois, I realised they had been working together until recently and she was more upset than I'd anticipated.

Some people can be a little too eager to pay tribute. One actor agreed that she would appear on *PM* to talk about a recently departed star and I asked, live on air, what it had been like to work with him. 'Oh darling, I never worked with him. Or met him. But he was a *marvellous* talent . . .'

19–25 June

ITV has offended me

I know Coronation Street *is different from real life*

I should warn you now: you might find parts of this column offensive.

Still reading? Perhaps you're a thrill-seeker determined that whatever I write in this family magazine is unlikely to offend a worldly-wise person like you. 'Throw whatever you've got at me, Mair. I sat through *The Prisoner* remake and I know no fear.'

Or maybe you're one of that special band of people who's prepared to be offended on behalf of others. More about them in a moment. But stand by please for the part of the column you might find offensive.

It relates to death. I realise that after a column pretty much devoted to death last week, more words on the subject would be about as welcome as Helen Thomas at a brit milah. But stay with me.

One of the last remaining stars of TV's *The Golden Girls,*

Rue McClanahan, died recently. She played Southern vamp Blanche 'her life is an open blouse' Devereaux. Her passing means her co-star Betty White is the last Golden Girl alive. Did you know that a few months back, when Ms McClanahan was hospitalised after a stroke, Betty White sent her a card, the contents of which were publicised at the time? The card read: 'Dear Rue, I hope you will hurry up and die so I can be the last Golden Girl left'.

It was obviously a joke, sent between two loving friends who shared a certain sense of humour. Perhaps some people were offended by it but, for me, unless Ms McClanahan was put out by it, what's it go to do with us?

The day after the shootings in Cumbria, Radio 4 broadcast an *Afternoon Play* that featured gunshot wounds and a killer who was heard yelling 'I'll put a bullet in your brain'. I didn't hear the play but there were scores of complaints and the BBC apologised, saying it should not have broadcast the play that day. ITV took no such chances with viewers' sensitivities. Its much-ballyhooed climax to a long-running *Coronation Street* storyline, which was to end with gunshots, bloodshed and death, was pulled from the schedule on the night of the killings and for the two nights that followed. 'Against the backdrop of Wednesday's tragic events in Cumbria, it would have been inappropriate to broadcast these episodes this week.' Normal service resumed five days after the real-life rampage. In last Monday's episode I watched a man kill another at point-blank range.

Who was right? Radio 4 offended some of its audience by broadcasting a play. ITV offended one viewer (me) by pulling a programme I was rather looking forward to. Was I horrified by the Cumbria shootings? Yes. Did I feel affected by them? Yes. But I have no trouble separating reality from TV drama, and was looking forward to the escapism. Programme controllers, though, have an entire audience to worry about – not just me.

On questions like this, is it right that anyone should speak for people affected by tragedy? If such people are offended by radio and TV coverage they consider insensitive or offensive, they can always speak up for themselves – and they should be heard. Similarly, any listener or viewer who is offended by something that's broadcast should shout and be heard. They deserve to be listened to and, in my experience at Radio 4, they are. Broadcasters make mistakes, and I can tell you we don't want to offend.

But please spare us from those people who profess to be offended on behalf of others: 'children might have been listening' – 'what if one of the relatives was watching?' – 'what if Rue McClanahan was upset by it?'

That's offensive.

24–30 July

Let's talk to the stars

All the best stories are hidden in the obits

Newspaper obituary columns can be huge fun. Not if you're in them, of course. Like filling in the last square of your Sudoku puzzle and finding the row has three sixes, your morning would be blighted by stumbling across news of your own demise.

I was once on a plane that was also carrying Michael Portillo (at the height of his powers) and James Naughtie. If this thing crashes, I thought, I'm going to be a footnote in the obituary columns, if I'm mentioned at all. After that,

I got into the habit of always checking the passenger list in
advance to make sure I'm the most famous person flying. It
pretty much means I get the train everywhere, since Alan
Yentob seems to be booked on every flight there is.

The bittersweet thing about obituaries (besides the obvious bitterness of someone dying) is that I often hear of
noteworthy people who somehow passed me by the entire
time they were alive. Matthew Bannister always has such
revelations on his obituary programme, *Last Words*, on
Friday afternoons on Radio 4. I used to catch the last five
minutes as I sat in the studio waiting to do a live trail at
4.30 for *PM*. Having caught the tail end of it for weeks and
discovered some fascinating people, I now make a point of
iPlayering it.

The *New York Times* does a nifty line in revealing obits and
I can highly recommend its tribute to another soul who falls
into the category of people I wish I'd known about when
they were alive. The headline hints at what's to come: 'Ed
Limato, Flashy Old-School Talent Agent to the Stars, Dies at
73'. There is a photo of Ed and he looks exactly like you think
he will. But read on: 'In an industry packed with over-the-
top personalities, the talent agent Ed Limato had no trouble
standing out. His typical work day started like this: clad in
a salmon-pink Richard James suit, he would charge into his
office and rattle his keys to his Aston Martin convertible in
a morning salute to his pet fish. Then, with a flourish of his
arm he would summon his three assistants by shouting "Let's
talk to the stars."' It's only the first paragraph and I love him
and miss him. I called my own agent (Bebe) to ask if she
knew Ed. Of course she was in a meeting but her email later
was sweet. She asked if I'd got the flowers she sent for my
marriage to Ruth Langsford.

World Cup fever – the repeat

I'm busy catching up with all the World Cup games I have stored in my PVR (personal video recorder) – watching each one in sequence.

It's tricky, steering clear of getting the results beforehand from the radio, the internet, Twitter, the radio, the television, the newspapers, the radio, word of mouth or through a Tiger Woods-style plane banner. But, so far, I have avoided every single World Cup result and can fully enjoy the taped games. I know England must have done well because I still see those little flags flying from cars. I have the Algeria game to watch tonight. My old friends Rodney Bewes and James Bolam are coming over to watch it with me. It'll be 3–0 to England, I reckon.

I hope the evening goes better than my dinner party last week at which two of my guests, Mel Gibson and Jon Gaunt, shouted at each other the entire time. What the Chief Rabbi made of it all he was too polite to say.

31 July–6 August

The trickle-down effect

Mandelson attempts another unauthorised leak

Is there something wrong with Lord Mandelson's bladder? I wouldn't usually raise such a sensitive issue, but since the good Lord has seen fit to reveal tiny details about his closest friends I feel no shame in going public about someone I barely know.

His memoir, *The Third Man*, has infuriated some Labour

colleagues (who are, I believe, pronouncing the title as an Irish person might). I was in the office when Lord Mandelson arrived to do his first big interview about the book, in the 8.10 a.m. slot on Radio 4's *Today*.

We all turned as he favoured the room with his arrival, and moved effortlessly, as if on castors, into the glass box where guests wait before they step, or in his case glide, into the studio. We all listened as the 8 a.m. news bulletin continued its comprehensive tour of the world, each of us taking bets as to which of the old political interview tricks he would employ during his chat.

Would it be the interruption of the first question in order to assert his authority? Or the faux laugh? Or how about the sudden apparent memory loss? In the end it was all three, but only after a troubling incident seconds before the interview. At around 8.07 a.m., I was aware of a kerfuffle. I turned to see Lord M striding – yes, using actual humanoid steps – towards the office door, which was still glowing with excitement at having been utilised by him moments before.

I instantly assumed this was an innovative trick from the master of spin to drum up more publicity for his tome – walking out of an interview before it's begun. What a masterstroke!

But as one of his entourage scurried after him I realised this was unplanned. I could hear Lord M ask something about where the toilet was. It was two minutes before he was due live on air and Lord Mandelson was going to spend a euro.

News of this surprise comfort break appeared to spread instantaneously. Suddenly, *Today* producers were sprinting after him.

I actually heard the air move as about five people gazelled towards Lord Mandelson to try to stop another of his ill-timed leaks. Their faces were contorted in horror. There may have been yelling. There was certainly a helluva racket as men and women hurtled towards a bemused Lord Mandelson, who was having it explained to him that 8.09 a.m. was no time to be fiddling with Peter.

He looked like a beslippered care-home resident who'd suddenly found himself in traffic. The throng of anxious producers led the former Secretary of State for Northern Ireland, the former Secretary of State for Trade and Industry, the former European Commissioner for Trade, to the studio. This was clearly no time for the former Secretary of State for Business, Innovation and Skills to be doing his business.

From my vantage point he was visibly back into gliding mode, and his countenance could be seen safely in studio S1. I may have detected his eyes darting around more than usual, perhaps looking for toilet facilities, but I can tell you they're pretty thin on the ground in there.

Listeners may have wondered why his laughter during the interview sounded especially strained. Or why he interrupted the first question before it actually began. Or why things seemed to slip his mind so readily.

But it's quite simple, really. Never broadcast on a full bladder.

14–20 August

I've been framed

My life has taken a turn I didn't see coming

I have asked the *Radio Times* people to amend the photograph that adorns the summit of my column. I want my photo to appear as though someone has crudely drawn a pair of specs on me. The reason? I want readers to get used to my new look – my new life, indeed. For, you see, I have reached the age where – gulp! – I need specs.

There, I've said it. Well, I've typed it. And if I increase the size of the font on this iPad I can read it too.

I'm mildly annoyed about this. I mean, I've long since accepted my physical shortcomings. My stomach is recognised by astronomers as having its own gravitational pull. My backside will not win Rear of the Year unless the award title is changed to the plural. I'm going slowly deaf in one ear and a podiatrist surprised me recently with the revelation that there is a webbed feature to my feet. I know. It made me feel queasy too, and they're my feet.

I was prepared to accept all of the above, but there's been something grating about the last six months, in which reading at close quarters has suddenly become impossible. At first I assumed it was the light in the room, or that small print was following the trend of small electronics products and just getting smaller.

Relaying this experience over dinner to a friend of similar vintage, she confessed to exactly the same phenomenon. Being a girl, however, she had done the sensible thing and gone to consult an optician. By her account he was a bit sneery, telling her that this suddenly failing vision was inevitable in her forties and no, it wouldn't get any better, thank you very much.

And so, at the age of forty-four, I stand on the brink of a new journey in life. I can see the horizon clearly, but this map is only visible at arm's length.

Today I'm going to visit an optician. I have no idea what to expect. The last time I had my eyes tested was at school, when my eyesight was so good I was able to read aloud not only every letter on the board, but also the details of the company that printed the card.

The world of eye-help is strange to me. You might as well ask me to go to a DIY store to ask for a specific item by name, or tell you what's happening in *Emmerdale*. The world is divided between the able-sighted and the be-glassed, and I'm about to learn a whole new way of being. Do they still have those cards with the gradually diminishing letters? What's the story with lenses? As someone who never carries a brolly or serious pen because he knows he will lose them, what's the likelihood I'll keep a pair of specs for more than a day? What shape and style of specs? Contact lenses? Disposables? Fluid? *String* for my glasses?

Sorry, I need to calm down. The truth is, I don't even know where to start. Are all opticians the same? Does going somewhere pricey mean I'll be happier or just poorer? Wait a second, what about laser surgery?

I really am off to the optician's now. And the only thing that brings me real comfort is the knowledge that however tough it's going to be for me in that shop, it's going to be much, much worse for them.

21–27 August

Female of the speccies

Those opticians are smarter than the average hack

There are things in life that I've spent too long thinking about. For example: those triangular signs you see on bridges that tell you the clearance height. Are they spot on or do they allow half an inch of grace? I wonder every time I see one, especially when I'm thundering through town in a forty-five-footer.

Similarly, when driving any motor vehicle, is there another warning light that comes on if you've spent fifty miles ignoring the low-fuel warning light? Perhaps a flashing red or violent orange that says: 'No, really, this time we mean it – you're about to grind to a halt.' I've never had the guts to find out.

I now have cause to consider a brand-new question. How often should you get something checked if it seems absolutely fine?

You'll recall that in last week's exciting episode my failing eyesight drove me to visit an optician for the first time. Actually, my failing eyesight drove me to an ironmonger, a shop selling flags and into a queue at a bus stop, but that's a whole other story. At the optician's I coped like a trouper with the phalanx of hi-tech equipment pointed at my peepers. The puffs of air, the flashing peripheral dots and a brilliant machine that takes 3D images of retinas. My eyes resemble bloodshot Neptunes.

But when the woman with the eye charts and a box full of lenses started filling in the paperwork, it all changed. 'When did you last have your eyes tested?' she asked.

I looked at my feet, at the wall, then back at the increasingly blurry eye chart whose third-last line had been shrouded in mystery only moments before. 'Um, I remember I was at school. I'm forty-four now, so shall we say thirty years ago?' I turned back to look at the optician. I was flushed with delight at having been able to subtract thirty from forty-four in my head but her mood had clearly changed and my flush changed hue to deep embarrassment. She couldn't have looked more appalled if I had told her: 'Your mother is a whore and your father is a bigamist.'

Her mouth fell open and her eyes widened. '*Thirty* years? Why so long?' I explained that I'd only had a problem in the past few months and that I didn't really see the need to check something on a regular basis that appeared to be functioning correctly. She asked whether I went to the dentist regularly for a check-up. Every six months, I told her, beaming and proffering the Happy Smile Badge I got at primary school, possibly around the same time as my last eye test. As soon as the words were out of my mouth I knew I'd fallen into a trap laid by this skilled optician who, I realised, could walk into a job as a smart-ass radio interviewer.

She managed to refrain from calling me an idiot to my face and explained that if I could take good care of my teeth every six months I really should get my eyes tested every couple of years. Later, as I browsed a rack of spectacles for the first time in my life (why do they all look the same?), I swear I could hear the words 'thirty years' wafting over from the reception desk. I fear I may be the talk of their Christmas party.

4–10 September

I don't do button-pushing

. . . not since that incident with the New York fireman

I like to think I'm a friend of technology. I've early-adopted more than Angelina Jolie. If it's new and shiny and really rather pointless, I'll be in the queue to buy it. I know what a cloud is and how it can store data, I'm a friend of the PAC code and I have no fear of multi-platform apps.

But I live in terror of digital recording equipment. And in my game that's a bad terror to have. It's like a nurse being afraid of blood, a Formula One driver who doesn't like fast cars, or a BBC executive in charge of moving to the north of England who doesn't want to move.

A little backstory first. It's September 2002 and I am in New York to make a *Broadcasting House* on the first anniversary of the attack on the Twin Towers. We've arranged an interview with a fire-fighter who was on duty that day and saved lives in one of the towers. My producer and I arrive at the fire station to meet this rather shy hero. I set my Sony Minidisc recorder whirring. No questions are required. For twenty-five searing minutes this quiet man calmly tells the most compelling, dramatic story I have ever heard. Factual, devoid of sentiment and powerful. I know this is going to make amazing radio. Almost half an hour has passed and a flashing battery symbol on the recorder tells me it's time to change the battery. I'm loath to stop him in full flow but interrupt and explain. Moments later, the battery changed, he finishes his story. He was brilliant.

A while later, back at the hotel, the producer and I realise that the act of changing the battery wiped that half-hour of interview. After some first-class swearing, we gingerly called the fire house to ask if he'd mind doing it again. He didn't mind, told the story exactly the same way and this time I left the button-pressing to my colleague.

Fast forward to August 2010 and *Radio Times* asks me to record an interview with a celebrity who'll be on the cover. The magazine has given me some sort of Dictaphone thing to record with. I get a demonstration of how to record and how to play it back. At the interview I do only the former. Such is my fear of wiping the recording accidentally, I (most unprofessionally) don't listen back to check if the words were there. For five days after the interview, the machine sits untouched in my bag. Only when *RT* takes it from me is it confirmed that the recording worked. Please don't mention my phobia or they won't ask me again.

I've been such a disappointment ...

Standing in for Mr Dimbleby on *Any Questions?* for the past fortnight has been fun, especially for the moments after the broadcast when audience members approach to say hello. Generally, these are people who like my work and it's very kind of them to stay on just to tell me that. But on one occasion a rather fierce-looking woman of a certain age marched up to the desk. The producer and I were rather startled by her sudden presence. 'I have to tell you I was *very* disappointed beforehand when I realised it wasn't going to be Jonathan Dimbleby, it was going to be you,' she began. I looked up to see a woman whose clothing said farmer's wife but whose voice said Princess Margaret. 'But I have to say, on balance, having been here for the entire programme,' (I was now eagerly anticipating a compliment) 'I still think he would have done a *much* better job.'

9–15 October

My bloody mouth

A gruesome tale of dental grime and neglect

Did you know it's now possible to buy a toothbrush that all but cleans your teeth for you? Electronic, of course. It tells you if you're pressing too hard. It has a separate display that indicates which quadrant of your mouth you should be cleaning and for how long. When you've done a full two minutes it vibrates pleasingly and the display shows a happy face. Can you believe that such a thing exists? What sort of mindless bloody idiot needs a SmartBrush to help them perform a simple task we all learn as children?

I bought my lovely new SmartBrush after a chilling visit to my lovely new dentist. The dentist I've been with for years kept cancelling appointments inexplicably, and after the third cancellation I thought, 'That's it – I'm taking my gob elsewhere'. I now realise he probably had a complete mental and physical breakdown on account of staring into my cavernous mouth once too often. Looking back, there were clues. His facial expression as he peered into my mouth always resembled that of a pathologist about to conduct a post-mortem after an especially grisly slaying.

What really opened my eyes to the true state of my mouth were the insightful questions of my new dentist. 'When did you last see the hygienist?' was the first indication that the paradise I believed existed in my babble-hole was lost. It was followed by 'How long do you take to clean your teeth?', then 'What do you want to do about all these cavities?', until finally stating – I think in a spirit of helpfulness – 'You mainly do radio, not TV, don't you? I don't suppose it matters too much.'

There was a whirlwind of X-rays and photographs. My old dentist tended to keep these to himself but the new chap insisted that I see them. Was he enjoying this?

I was shown a close-up of the grime surrounding the teeth of a heavy smoker whose mouth had not been hindered by fluoride in about twenty years. How can people like that live with themselves, I wondered. It transpires the teeth in the image were mine. Another snap was a close-up of a mountain range on Mars – the fiery red planet. No, they were my gums. And what about this captivating shot of the Grand Canyon? It transpires my teeth have bigger gaps than a season of Harold Pinter plays and more holes than Phil Spector's defence case.

Next week I have a double appointment – a *double* appointment, that is – with the hygienist. I'm not sure who I feel more sorry for, her or me. On the plus side, the new toothbrush is working a treat, though its complex instructions are correct to warn there may be some bleeding. It's hard to describe quite how much blood there's been. Have you seen *Dexter*?

BBC industrial action: my plea

There is a strike planned at the BBC on Tuesday 5 and Wednesday 6 October. I wasn't going to draw attention to it. It's far too serious a subject to be discussed here, and to write about it would demand an understanding of pension schemes and, of course, no one understands pension schemes. Since I will be on strike both days, I would ask that you don't break the strike by reading these words until at least Thursday 7 October.

23–29 October

Skip to my loo

When it comes to quality WCs, you can't beat Sky

And so there I was at the Cheltenham Literary Festival. You weren't expecting that, were you? In the category of sentences you don't ever expect to hear, it's up there with 'and the winner is Ann Widdecombe' or 'and now the final episode of *Coronation Street*'.

Admittedly, I wasn't there to talk about my own literary achievements. The organisers chose to ignore this fine column and disregarded my only published book, *The Art of the Interview: Reconsidering the Awkward Silence*. Instead, they asked me to host two discussions at the festival, because Mariella Frostrup can't be everywhere, despite how it looks.

The highlight was the Writers' Room. Or was it the Writer's Room? I can't remember, which is proof that I didn't belong there. It's the place where participants can relax and chat before and after their events. A sort of business-class lounge for people with publishers. I marched up to the reception desk and announced my presence. The woman didn't flinch and her friendly smile didn't crack, but there was something (was it in the eyes?) that said 'what the hell are you doing here?' A brightly coloured plastic tag was attached to my wrist. I said to Virginia Ironside* that it made me feel like I was at a rock festival. She said it made her feel like we were in hospital, waiting for an operation. I put that down to the fact her session was about bereavement.

I looked round the room and didn't recognise anybody.

I put on my glasses, looked round the room and saw Michael Cockerell* and Germaine Greer.* I wondered how she'd reacted on being told she had to wear a plastic wrist tag. I suddenly had an overwhelming desire to pee. This was nothing to do with Ms Greer, it's just my age. I was directed out the back of the Writer's/rs' Room through what I can only describe as a lavishly appointed tent. It had fine carpeting and better furniture than I've ever owned. I immediately feared I had been excluded from a first-class

---

* Sorry about all the name-dropping.

lounge for people with publishers, but the presence of television cameras indicated that this was where Sky did their stuff. The loo to which I'd been directed was, I guess, part of their set-up.

Upon entering, I realised I'd never been in such a plush portable toilet. And I hadn't even been yet. I've stayed in five-star hotels with less attractive WCs. There was tiling, lighting, decent mirrors, top-quality liquid soap (two kinds), two sinks and a lavatory that was so spotless Kenneth Williams wouldn't have baulked at using it.

I emerged giddy with excitement, my hands stinking of jojoba and parsnips. And this was the moment when I met for the first time the new controller of BBC Radio 4, my recently appointed boss, Gwyneth Williams. I hadn't expected to encounter her until later in the day and was slightly blind-sided. The only thing on my mind was how fantastic the Sky toilets were but I sensed it would be wrong to begin our working relationship with that. I managed to say something congratulatory about her appointment and she said something about how nice it was to meet me and thanked me for my brilliant presentation of *Front Row*.

30 October–5 November

This is Moscow calling

Is technology robbing us of some of radio's oldest delights?

You might consider that an odd question. Not as odd as 'Did the sideboard harpoon Hattie Jacques's spleen?', I'll grant you, but odd nonetheless. The internet, WiFi and shiny hand-held devices mean the world's radio stations are available to us as never before. What jazz are they playing in New Orleans right now? Tune in from your kitchen. What are the top stories in Adelaide? Find out on the bus. The variety and excitement of the planet's broadcasters are in the palm of your hand and, truly, it's a wonder of our age. And there's more to come: last week the radio industry in the UK announced details of the Radioplayer – an online system that will bring together dozens of UK radio stations. I love all that.

And yet . . .

Come with me, if you will, to my bedroom at home as a teenager (sorry about the smell, and those magazines aren't mine), and feast your eyes on that magnificent radio/cassette recorder by the bed. If younger readers are now googling 'cassette recorder' they can get lost. This silver and black dynamo can not only tune in to three different frequencies, but by putting a blank cassette into the recorder I can record programmes and play them back when I like. How amazing is that?

On a clear night, if I position the red line perfectly, I can pick up – brace yourself – commercial radio from Edinburgh! More exotically, there is the midnight news on what I think is called the Radio Moscow World Service, with its chimes from the Kremlin. In between – and often at the same time – a myriad of stern-sounding Germans, romantic French and talkative Italians all talking gibberish.

It doesn't sound like much, I realise, but it's where I first met radio and we've been together ever since. Years later, on an episode of *Life on Mars*, I spotted my old radio/cassette recorder in the background of a scene. I'm not ashamed to admit that I rewound the recording and freeze-framed the picture and stared at it – lost in personal memories while admiring the set designer's deep understanding of the era.

Which brings me to last weekend, as I drove round north

Wales for the first time. (Side note: it's prettier than you can imagine; Caernarfon – lovely; Menai suspension bridge – eye-wateringly beautiful; Portmeirion – are they on something?) In a new area it's always fun to sample the radio and there was lots of good stuff to choose from, commercial and BBC. But you know what made me whoop? Twiddling the dial in the old-fashioned way and stumbling across RTÉ Radio all the way from Ireland ... from Ireland, that is! I ditched all the fine Welsh stations to hear the Irish accents, adverts and news, and stayed with it until the Welsh mountains silenced the last audible word. And here's the perverse thing: had I been driving around Ireland and picked up BBC Radio Wales I would have followed it just as eagerly.

New technology has opened my ears to fantastic stations around the globe and, hand on heart, I'd rather live in today's radio world than the one of my childhood. Best of all, radio is a medium that's growing while others struggle.

But I fear that amid all the brilliant technology, we might lose the magic of skimming up and down the dial and making the accidental radio discovery and— [Column interrupted by someone speaking Russian.]

4–10 December

And the award goes to

It's time to stop wasting money on these jamborees

I'd like to draw the sting of criticisms that will follow this week's column by using that tired and not very effective technique: listing the criticisms myself first. Here they are:

1: Aren't you pulling up the ladder after you?

2: Have you forgotten the less well-known people who deserve widespread recognition?

3: If you really want to save the BBC money shouldn't you resign, you big waste of space?

I will deal with all three of those points at the end of this article. Possibly upside down like a crossword solution, just to make it interesting. But for now, if indeed you're still reading this, you're probably wondering what's on my mind. It boils down to this: the BBC should pull out of awards ceremonies.

The genesis of this heresy was a couple of years ago, when I was told that you have no chance of winning the UK's top radio award unless you paid. I assumed bribery was required and reached instinctively for my wallet but it transpired that the awards – in common with virtually all such jamborees in radio and TV – needed you to pay just to submit an entry. And then, if you were lucky enough to be nominated, you had to pay handsomely for each place at the table in the giant ballroom for the ceremony itself.

On the one hand, you can understand why. Those vol-au-vents won't serve themselves. And the glory of an award can lift the spirits in a way that's rivalled only by true love, or seeing a rival fail to win an award. You can't put a price on that. But things have changed.

Until the other week, the BBC was swimming in cash. In fact, I was in the money jacuzzi on the ninth floor with the director-general, almost drowning in an ocean of fifties, when he got the call from David Cameron saying – and I'm quoting directly – 'The game's up, beardy, get your cheque book'.

In a place like the BBC, awards must cost a lot of money. Just take those radio awards. Each programme can submit multiple entries every year. Multiply that by all the programmes and stations across the UK. Add to that the cost of the staff who are removed from making programmes to compile entries. It must be thousands of pounds. And that's just for one radio awards ceremony.

I realise that to withdraw from all awards ceremonies would rob talented people of industry-wide national recognition – particularly those in local broadcasting. Who am I to say others shouldn't have that morale-boosting excitement? Another thought occurs: what about the effect on commercial broadcasters? If they're not winning awards in competition with the BBC, won't it all end up like a boycotted Olympics?

So to deal with those three questions from earlier (I can't work out how to change my font, never mind type upside down).

1: It does look like that.
2: No, but it tends to be bosses rather than minions who go to awards ceremonies.
3: Yes, you're right.

As you can tell, I have no answers to the problems my suggestion creates. But I do know that I have no will to see creative people made redundant as a result of the new licence-fee settlement while we carry on paying to win awards.

11–17 December

Festive greetings

The hell(o)ish dividing line that separates the nation

Hello. I hope that greeting didn't startle you. Did you say it back? In recent months I've chronicled my rapid decline into crumbly old age. My failing eyesight and decaying mouth are both signs that I won't see forty again. Here's another – I've started walking. Not the everyday kind that I began to master as a toddler; I mean proper Walking. Weatherproof boots. Sturdy jacket. Maps. Compass. Countryside. No doubt there are plenty of younger people who Walk, but in my imagination it was always rather dull middle-aged people who would find Walking interesting. In other words, me. I'm not terribly fast or anything and don't scale any great heights. It's not as if they'll be asking me to present *Countryfile*. Not at my age.

But for the past three or four years I've been tramping along public footpaths in remote parts of the kingdom which previously I'd have whizzed by in the car or train. And I've learned that one of the great unwritten rules of Walking is that you should greet Walkers coming from the opposite direction. I've lost count of the number of times ruddy-faced, big-booted people have cheerily wished me 'Good morning', 'Lovely day' or 'Get out of the way, fatso, you're spoiling the view for everyone'.

It won't be news to you that people in towns and cities tend not to greet strangers with a welcoming 'Hello'. But did you know that there is a 'hello' dividing line that separates the proper countryside from not only towns but also the big open spaces of country parks? Don't bother the Ordnance Survey people about their omission – the line is invisible. I've been in a few of those beautiful country parks recently – they're a bit more manicured than normal countryside and they're full of people out for a stroll. But if you say hello to any of them, as I have done, they look at you as if you're bonkers. I've stopped saying it now. Not least because I overheard one of them saying to her friend, 'I think that was Eddie Mair. He's a complete walker.'

Christmas is a-comin'

The fact that this edition of *Radio Times* has been published weeks before the programmes in it will be aired can mean only one of two things. Either the editor has been socialising with Paul Gascoigne again and has lost several days, or Christmas is coming. Thanks to my extensive contacts, I am able to reveal here some Christmas morning highlights:

Radio 4: Evan Davis and Sarah Montague present a special edition of *Today*, live from a children's hospital. Every child gets a gift. This, being Radio 4, cannot be a plastic toy or even free batteries – it's a copy of *A History of the World in 100 Objects*.

Radio 2: Paul O'Grady's three-hour morning special will have top tips to make your Christmas even more lovely, with musical treats and a raft of mystery celebrity callers. Oh, and Paul will be urging listeners to take to the streets in his fight against government oppression.

Radio 1: Join Chris Moyles for his personal re-interpretation of Charles Dickens's *A Christmas Carol* in which Chris plays all the parts except that of Ebenezer Scrooge, which is played by the BBC.

2011

Behind closed doors

What really goes on when BBC presenters hook up

It was a pleasure to welcome back Miriam O'Reilly to the fold at last week's meeting of BBC presenters. You're probably not aware of such a gathering, as its existence and membership are not known to outsiders . . . a bit like the Mafia or the Freemasons, or the George Osborne Fan Club.

For the past ten years, we've been meeting once a month at 6 p.m. in a secret location in Television Centre under the name 'The 1922 Committee' (because no one is sober after about twenty past seven). The purpose is to discuss, in an open and non-judgemental forum, issues that matter only to presenters: make-up tips, arguments about the most flattering lighting – that sort of thing. I've no idea what the telly presenters talk about.

Entry is open to anyone with an on-screen or on-air role at the BBC and almost everyone attends, with a few notable exceptions. Jonathan Ross only came to one meeting and didn't come back after an incident. Martha Kearney from Radio 4's *The World at One* has been barred on account of always being surrounded by bees. At first, everyone was grateful for the free honey and there was some snickering the day Jonathan Ross got stung. But after the terrible time when a swarm got a whiff of whatever's keeping Melvyn Bragg's hair in place and homed in on his barnet, Martha's had to make do with the newsletter updates. To my dying day I will never forget his screams: 'Not my crowning glory, not my crowning glory!'

But I digress. At last week's meeting there was agreement on the items on the agenda. 1: Aren't we all terrific? 2: Aren't things going downhill but for our unstinting work? 3: Shouldn't we all be paid a good deal more for being so marvellous?

Those are the only three items ever on the agenda and they're always agreed unanimously. Just as we were turning our attention to the informal part of the evening (tip: don't say yes if Jeremy Paxman offers to show you one of his card tricks) someone piped up asking about sexism and ageism at the BBC. I think it was one of the older girls. She pointed out that Miriam had that very day won a famous victory over the Corporation with regard to ageism and that perhaps we should consider the issues raised. Well, as you'll have gathered from my descriptions, the 1922 is not a venue for serious discussions. While we were all happy for Miriam, the suggestion that we should interrupt our festivities stopped the party dead in its tracks. The clarion call caused Jeremy to lose concentration mid-riffle and he spent the rest of the evening playing fifty-two-card pick-up.

At that moment Miriam herself arrived. There was applause, cheers and an ill-fated solo attempt to carry her shoulder-high, which only stopped when Kirsty Young finally admitted she couldn't manage it as she'd slipped a disc. 'Was it a Desert Island Disc?', twenty-seven smartarse presenters piped up in unison. Sometimes we're our own worst enemies.

My feud with Robert Peston

I realise that as a result of being the top-trending Twitter topic for a week, and the acres of newsprint devoted to the subject, you've turned to this column for my take on my ongoing bitter and angry feud with Robert Peston. As you can see, I am out of space but I will return to the subject.

16–22 April

I'm a celebrity

My fame is growing – and, yes, I do look like this

Standing in again for Jonathan Dimbleby on Radio 4's *Any Questions?* for the past fortnight. This gives me the chance to meet my public face to face, and for the public to mutter to each other 'He doesn't look anything like he sounds'. Mind you, in Ashford the other week I had several autograph hunters who professed to being big fans.

Oh yes. You get some idea of my stratospheric stardom when you read the following genuine tweet that was pointed out to me afterwards by a friend: 'I got Eddie Mair's autograph. I didn't realise how good that is until I looked him up on Wikipedia.'

19:22 and all that

Another lively meeting of the 1922 Committee, the secret gathering of BBC presenters that gets its name from the fact no one is sober after twenty past seven. It used to be such a convivial get-together. Presenters could let their hair down – or take it off completely – in a carefree atmosphere. Changed days.

I arrived a little late, to find Rav Wilding taking witness statements from everyone as a bloodied Michael Buerk was administered a recuperative brandy by Barbara Windsor. Someone had tried to beat him unconscious with a copy of the *Guardian*. Monty Don was being shouted at for letting the pot plants die, and over in the corner the party for presenters going to Salford fell flat when he left early.

I'm Eddie, media personality for hire

Like a supermarket trolley, I tend to move in small circles. Almost all my broadcasting work is confined to news. I don't go to showbusiness parties after an incident in which Kate Adie mistook me for a waiter and demanded I get chef to rustle up some beer-battered curly fries. In fact, if it wasn't for my tireless but completely secret charity work, I would hardly see a soul. So it was a shock to find myself suddenly appearing as one third of a panel on a pilot for a TV quiz show last week.

I say suddenly because I only got the call five days before the recording. This clearly means the three first choices dropped out through diary clashes, illness or death. But I'm not proud, and when my agent rang me excitedly to tell me about the proposal ('Eamonn, I've finally got you a gig you won't have to do with that bloody wife of yours') I thought, why not?

I think there's probably an unwritten rule about blabbing the details of a pilot programme. So although I could name-drop like a Buckingham Palace private secretary, I will refrain. Except to say that, in make-up, Jimmy Carr asked me my views on Libya. And then he told me I don't look anything like I sound.

I learnt two things as a result of the pilot:

1. Don't go on a panel with two professional comedians. You'll spend your time laughing at them and anything you have to say will be extremely unfunny.
2. I never knew this: comedians don't like doing corporate events. I'd assumed that being paid twenty grand a time for telling gags to drunk executives would be the icing on the comedic cake. But my fellow panellists try to avoid them. The audience is not there to see you. They talk through your act and generally have their backs to you. That was a surprise to this journalist.

On the other hand, a good comedian would have found a way of ending that true story with a witty punchline.

23–29 April

Stick to the point

How (not) to give a concise answer . . .

Hello. What's the point I'd like to make? Well, for half an hour every week Radio 4 throws open the airwaves to its listeners for *Any Answers?*, the live, uncompromising phone-in show hosted by award-winning talk radio DJ Gary Bellamy. No, wait a minute, that's Radio 4's *Down the Line*. *Any Answers?* is the listeners' opportunity to respond to *Any Questions?*, the live topical programme in which the public can use thoughtful questions to gently probe four panellists.

Jonathan Dimbleby is, of course, the host, but sometimes when he's away they ask me to fill in. Actually, I consider that I am filling in for the late Nick Clarke, who used to fill in for Jonathan. It's sort of comforting to think that Nick is just unavailable, as opposed to deceased. For the same reason I cannot delete his phone numbers from my mobile. Do you do that? But I digress. For the past couple of weeks I've been filling in for Nick/Jonathan and, as usual, it's been fun.

There is always a small dinner before the programme, in a restaurant near the venue. This has three purposes. It provides a logistical buffer so that panellists coming from hither, and, indeed, thither, can arrive in good time for the programme. Second, it allows everyone to get to know one another. And third, it means we can ply the guests with cheap wine to get them loose-lipped, controversial and headline-grabbing! I'm joking, of course. The wine is not cheap.

Where was I? Oh, yes. I slightly put my foot in it with regard to alcohol at a recent dinner. One of the panellists asked where Jonathan was. At that point I wasn't sure whether he was just on holiday or working on another landmark documentary (it was the latter, I learnt later). Instead of being honest, I fell into a familiar trap of trying to be funny and making up a complete lie. I replied that he was in a drying-out facility. I expected her to laugh or at least tell me not to be so stupid, but instead she looked a bit startled.

Later in the meal she leant in to enquire of me, *sotto voce*: 'Gosh, I'd no idea about Jonathan. When is he expected to get out?'

But I digress again. Please stop trying to interrupt me. *Any Answers?* is a simple format: just the host and the listeners – with the emphasis on allowing the listeners to talk. It's a programme that seems to divide people. 'Who was that lunatic rambling on for ages this afternoon?' people often ask when I've been especially loquacious. Others believe some of the callers have a screw loose, while still more believe it's the most sensible half-hour on the radio.

Wait, what was my point? Hello? Yes. Having done about a million phone-ins, and not being prone to exaggeration, I can tell you that the last Saturday I did *Any Answers?* something happened to me that has never happened before. How can I put this in a way that won't put you off your tea? About an hour before we went on air, I developed a sudden health problem that ... wait. We're out of time? I'll call in again next week.

More embarrassment

Lunch last week with Piers Morgan, Moussa Koussa, Laurent Gbagbo and Jeremy Clarkson. Very embarrassing moment when the waiter came over to tell us that as a result of numerous complaints from other deeply offended diners, Piers would have to leave.

30 April–6 May

Time and motions

Presenting live radio drives me round the U-bend

At the end of last week's exciting episode, I left readers on tenterhooks over my last edition of *Any Answers?*. Once my bosses read this, they could very well decide it was my last edition. But I believe passionately that you turn to me for the sort of behind-the-scenes insight into radio that no one else will bring you. And I confidently predict that you won't read about this anywhere else. Ready?

Any Answers? is a half-hour-long phone-in on Saturday afternoons on Radio 4. It's just the presenter and callers. I often worry about being late for it. After all, if I don't show up at the last minute, the programme is in trouble. So far, my attendance record is unblemished.

But last time, just before I left home to go to the studio, I felt a gurgling. Perhaps you have experience of the gurgling I mean. Not the satisfying gurgle of a meal being digested. Not the happy sound of the body functioning as it should. This gurgling made me more anxious than a *News of the World* reporter in a police station.

A few moments later, having taken decisive action, I emerged from the loo, still with the uneasy feeling that the gurgling would return. I won't say I knew it in my water because at that moment I appeared to be 100 per cent water, but you know I do have some psychic powers. Richard Hammond could have saved himself weeks in hospital if he'd taken my call. In any event, I set off in the car wearing an adult diaper. Not really, but if I'd had one I'd have worn it.

As sure as eggs is eggs (was it eggs causing this? No, they clog you up, don't they?) I was less than a mile from Broadcasting House when the gurgling returned with an unexpected urgency. I wondered where the toilet facilities were on London's Marylebone Road. Would the queue at Madame Tussaud's step willingly aside for an anxious Scotsman hurtling towards the lavs? Like the trouper I am, I held on and ran like a gazelle through the doors of BH. In truth, I probably shambled like an arthritic hippo, but in my mind everything was urgency.

I made use of the impeccable toilet facilities twice more in the space of twenty-five minutes. It didn't stop the gurgling and its calamitous effects. What's worse, my anxiety about being locked in the studio for half an hour, solely responsible for the network, was only adding to the gurgling. I was more nervous than a News International executive before a committee of MPs.

With thirty minutes to go, I decided there was only one thing for it. I would have to be honest with the producer. That is *never* the right thing to do, of course, but this was an emergency. I didn't want to add to her editorial burden, but thought she'd want a warning so she would have a few minutes to think about her options, should I sprint to the loo while we were on air. It's the sort of thing they ask potential producers at job interviews. 'It's five minutes to transmission and your presenter shows up drunk – what do you do?' (The correct answer is take them to the bar and try to catch up with them.)

Naturally, my producer knew exactly what to do. She told me sternly that if I didn't get my downstairs stuff in order right away, she would ensure I never worked in broadcasting again.

Worked better than any pill. I recommend it.

7–13 May

Hang on, I've got a plan

What to do when Any Questions? *is cancelled . . .*

I was at a high-security drying-out facility recently when I began to get text messages from concerned friends. 'Are you OK?'

I know you're shocked. How did I manage to smuggle a mobile phone into a high-security drying-out facility? Let's just say that I subsequently needed to spend some time in a higher-security medical facility The point is that, shortly after 8 p.m. on the Friday in question, dexterous texters were in a finger-pushing frenzy demanding to know why *Any Questions?* wasn't on air.

Given my incarceration in the Any Questions Drying-out Facility, I was unable to advise, but upon my release I learnt that trouble on the East Coast Main Line had stranded three-quarters of the panel at a poorly stocked station Lite Bite.

They passed the time evenly distributing the remaining two sandwiches, but it wasn't the evening they'd prepared for. Meanwhile, back at the venue in County Durham, the broadcast had to be cancelled. I could only imagine the calamity and frantic phone-calling. In contrast, serenity reigned in my secure environs, bar the occasional moaning of my room-share, a radio presenter from the east coast who was mainlining.

Radio 4 had three options when it realised *AQ?* wouldn't make it to air:

1. Go ahead with the sole available panellist, Professor Richard Grayson.

2. Switch format, allowing Professor Grayson to quiz the audience about Libya, the Alternative Vote and the Common Agricultural Policy.
3. Broadcast the stand-by programme.

Yes, although it's thought *Any Questions?* has never previously been cancelled in its sixty-year history, that didn't mean the people in Radio 4 continuity were not prepared. No siree. Those people have a swivel-eyed determination to plan for every eventuality and are dedicated to the smooth running of the world's finest speech-radio network.

Power cut at Broadcasting House? No worries. Radio 4 continuity will magically pop up from another location without missing a beat. Aliens attacking Earth? Radio 4 will be ready with a timely re-broadcast of *The War of the Worlds* in *Book at Bedtime*. Intercontinental ballistic missiles destined to destroy the United Kingdom within four minutes? Tune in for a reassuring *Thought for the Day*.

With that level of preparedness, broadcasting crises hold no fear for the Radio 4 continuity team. Most live programmes have a taped backup ready to be transmitted at a moment's notice. We checked this out on *PM* the other day. Should *The Food Programme* become voiceless because Sheila Dillon's having an emergency Heimlich manoeuvre, there's a recorded show about puddings in the can (that's the programme, not the puddings). If Mark Lawson on *Front Row* should run out of things to say, he will pop up on tape talking about creative writing.

So you see, it's not just about avoiding dead air; these continuity people even do their best to ensure there's a match-up between the content and tone of the missing live programme and the recorded replacement.

I made the mistake of asking what the replacement for *PM*

is, should I fail to sober up one evening, and it appears to be
an hour-long tribute to Mel Blanc.

21–27 May

Meet, greet 'n' bleat

When the boss calls, my brain goes missing

In Radio 4's *PM* office last week we had a tip-off that Sir
Chris – correction: Lord Patten of Hong Kong – was going
to pay us a visit. He's now the chairperson of the BBC Board
of Governors. No, that can't be right. I think it's the Trust
now. Wait. Is he chairperson of that, or is there a new title?
Hang on, I'm going to search online.

Ah yes, I knew all this really. 'Lord Patten of Barnes has
been appointed chairman of the BBC Trust with effect from
1 May 2011.' The Trust website quotes him as saying, 'The
BBC is the best broadcasting organisation in the world, and
it is a great privilege to have been asked to take some responsibility for keeping it that way for the next four years. I look
forward to finding out for myself just what the bloody hell
they think they're playing at on Radio 4.'

News of his unannounced visit spread round the office like
the Ebola virus, with similar effects. It's always like this when
we know someone important's due. We ought to be able to
just carry on as normal because that's what visitors want to
see. Yet we end up doing one of those stagey versions of a
newsroom you see in every TV drama about a newsroom.

I'm no longer Eddie Mair, who's presenting *PM*. I morph
into 'Eddie Mair as "Eddie Mair who's presenting *PM*"',
suddenly conscious of everything I'm doing. Is this chair

at the right height? Pen in hand or behind my ear? Which paper should I pretend to be reading? Should I be wearing my headphones? What about wearing my headphones and making a phone call? Too much? Not enough? Will someone please *direct* me? It's so hot in here. MAKE-UP!

Like the shopkeeper in *Mr Benn*, Lord Patten suddenly appears in the room, apparently from nowhere. Everyone in the office is in the same mode as me. No one acknowledges our visitor is there and each individual is furiously engaged in the act of appearing relaxed and nonchalant, yet busy and productive. It's not an easy thing for non-actors to pull off. There are lots of furrowed brows, some slightly shouty phone conversations, yet not a single swearword. The intensity of it all makes some people quietly wet themselves.

Soon, I am standing up, being introduced to the good Lord, hoping he doesn't notice the damp patch. While I embark on my famously witty small talk ('I met you in Hong Kong.' Silence. 'You probably don't remember.'), an unintroduced man behind the chairman is writing notes that I assume will subsequently form part of my letter of dismissal. Is the scribbly man finalising where the budget cuts will come? Is he noting Lord Patten's sandwich order? His anonymous presence lurks while the Trust chairman listens with fascination as I hold forth on topics as varied as the capture of bin Laden, the Greek bailout and my long-term vision for the BBC.

Well, those are the topics on which 'Eddie Mair as "Eddie Mair who's presenting *PM*"' had planned to do some improv. The reality, I fear, involved some mumbling and looking at my shoes. Looking at his shoes, then back to my shoes.

That's probably what happened, but like meeting royalty, it's over in moments. And like meeting royalty, I can't remember much about it, except for my bowing and scraping.

28 May–3 June

Alvin's stardust

Soft soap gives me the nicest hands in radio

The American financial adviser Alvin Hall paid a visit to the *PM* studio recently and told me just before we went live that I had lovely hands. Literally no one had ever said those words to me before. At that moment I looked down at my fat, wrinkled, sausage-like digits and examined them in the light of this startling compliment. My, they looked old. When did I last really look at them? I swear that last time I really looked at them they were wrinkle-free. Was that a liver spot?

I think I said to Alvin something like 'Seriously?', which upon reflection was just an invitation for him to repeat the compliment, which thankfully he did. And then I think I said that literally no one had ever said those words to me, and then I think the red light came on and we spent the next four minutes talking about the price of gold. I don't remember what we said about gold because all the time I was thinking for the first time in my life about the aesthetic qualities of my hands and whether they merited the moniker 'lovely'.

As you can tell, this compliment has stayed with me and I have given some thought as to why that unusual moment took place. I believe there are a number of workable possibilities.

One, Alvin has a highly developed sense of humour.

Two, Alvin is a nice person who was taught to always find something nice to say about someone. Arriving in the studio that afternoon he surveyed the damage that life has caused to my physical appearance over the years, and kindly complimented the only part of me that would not be immediately condemned by council inspectors as unfit for human habitation.

Three, it was a bet – the details of which will appear in Alvin's weekly column, 'Finance Head', in *American Financial Adviser Times*.

Four, he really did think I have lovely hands.

Now, as I stare at the back of my great-grandmother's hands as they type these words, I ponder point four. I realise that being complimented on your appearance by a financial expert is akin to a beautician swooning over your perfectly completed tax return.

But, as you can tell, a small part of me (not my huge fingers, obviously) believes point four, and my agent is already investigating hand-modelling assignments with Saga and the British Institution of Embalmers.

My plan for an eight-day week

May is fine, but I do miss April, when there was a public holiday every week. Can't we go back to that? Having every Monday off work was fun. Mind you, I suppose we need to have a reason to down tools once a week, otherwise it's just laziness, isn't it? Well, there's always a saint to celebrate and the Vatican seems to be rushing out new ones every five minutes. Or we could have a three-day weekend to marvel at the presenters and panels on whatever new show Simon Cowell has out this week.

I've always harboured the secret thought that if we simply added an extra day to come between Sunday and Monday, we could take that off without relinquishing the five-day working week. In my mind it seems brilliantly feasible, but whenever I suggest it I'm told it would play havoc with the Earth's rotation, horoscopes and Monday's editions of *Coronation Street*, and could I just shut up and get another round in?

Azerbaijan

Seriously, where is it?

9–15 July

All change at R4

My brilliant idea to shake up the schedules*

Radio 2 recently had a fun old time with its 2Day – a '12-hour on-air celebration of everything the UK's favourite radio station has to offer'. They threw Tony Blackburn and Trevor Nelson on air together. Ken Bruce and Bob Harris also became a double act for an hour. People seemed to like it and I'm sure for Radio 2 it was a fun way of getting people to sample the network.

I have an even better idea for Radio 4. To be honest, it's not strictly speaking my idea, it belongs to the Radio 4 newsreader Vaughan Savidge. Vaughan, by the way, is affectionately known as Prawn Sandwich. It's because he smells of prawns.

It's not really the done thing to praise colleagues publicly. We're British and everyone finds it embarrassing, even if it is well-intentioned. But I must say it: not only does Vaughan

---

* With apologies to Vaughan Savidge.

read the news impeccably, he's also a delight to work with. Too much of a delight sometimes. No one gets me closer to corpsing on air than Vaughan. When I know he's doing the news on *PM*, I expect, and get, an hour of being close to the titter-edge. He, on the other hand, can hold it together no matter the provocation. He's very good.

There, that's the embarrassing praise out of the way. Thank goodness Vaughan never reads this column. Should you be reading this by accident, Vaughan, you're a talentless, no-good bum.

What's Vaughan's idea? Brace yourself. Move all Radio 4's programmes around for a day. Ta-da. I love it. Imagine the anarchy!

The programmes themselves would all do what they always do. *Today* would be three hours of news and current affairs. *The Food Programme* would still talk about food. The only thing that would change would be the time of day they're on air. So often I hear from listeners who say, 'Oh, I never hear the first half-hour of *PM*' (I think that may have been the Radio 4 controller) and others who have never heard *Woman's Hour* because it's on at the wrong time for them. (I think that may have been the Radio 4 controller too.)

These days, there are lots of funky ways to listen to shows you miss, but it's hard to beat the pleasure of live listening. Imagine something out of the ordinary shaking up your listening patterns.

Here's my draft schedule for Monday just gone. You get the idea. What would you do?

0600: *PM*
0700: *Woman's Hour*
0800: *The World at One*
0830: *I'm Sorry I Haven't a Clue*

0900: *The Archers*
0915: *Woman's Hour Drama*
0930: *The Infinite Monkey Cage*
1000: *Front Row*
1030: *Book of the Week*
1045: *Book at Bedtime*
1100: *Yesterday in Parliament*
1130: *Quote . . . Unquote*
1200: *Six O'Clock News*
1230: *The Food Programme*
1300: *Today*
1600: *Start the Week*
1700: *The World Tonight*
1745: *The Archers*
1800: *Midnight News*
1830: *Material World*
1900: *Start the Week*
1945: *The Making of Music*
2000: *Today in Parliament*
2030: *Yesterday in Parliament*
2100: *Off the Page*
2130: *The Private Lives of British Pakistanis*
2200: *You and Yours*
2300: *Analysis*
2330: *Afternoon Play*
0015: *The Making of Music*

16–22 July

Signs of madness

Ridiculous warnings are driving me crazy . . .

Don't read this column while baking a cake. Don't read this column while performing open-heart surgery. Don't read this column if you don't speak English. This rather pointless advice will be explained in a moment.

Visiting Scotland at the weekend – as my parole officer allows twice a year – I was struck by a number of things:

1. The number of students from England fleeing back south across the border;
2. How there are literally no Scottish voices on radio in Scotland because they're all working in London;
3. And how odd the road signs are.

I don't mean the classic 'man having trouble with the umbrella' or the 'stunt motorbike flying over the car'. I mean the large electronic signs whose constantly changing messages are, I imagine, controlled by a mad-eyed goon in a spaceship, but are in all probability the work of a kindly civil servant in Edinburgh.

In and around London these signs are always warning of accidents ahead causing three-hundred-mile tailbacks. These warnings always appear just as you reach the tailback, five yards after the last possible turn-off. On less deadly occasions, they will alert you to the fact that it's fifteen miles, or eighteen minutes, to the M4. It's very important to know how close you are to the M4. Why don't you check now, just to be on the safe side?

But the signs I witnessed in Fife, Perth and Kinross, and Angus were of a different nature. Perhaps because these beautiful areas are rarely in thrall to the traffic queue, the signs are put to a different use. I have no trouble with one message I saw: don't drink and drive. There was another warning of the dangers of taking drugs and driving. Again, hard to argue with the sense of that. Another warned of the dangers of adjusting your satnav while driving. Fair enough.

Last time I visited there was a sign saying 'Check your fuel'. I immediately averted my eyes from the road to find the fuel gauge on my hire car. By the time I looked up I'd crashed into the back of a car full of English students who'd just arrived for the free education. Not really. But I did wonder what business it was of the road sign to ask how much fuel I have.

On this visit, a new gem: 'Take extra care while towing'. I'm not making this up.

For me, this goes beyond solid public-service information and wanders over the highway like a drunk driver, crossing the line into the realm of useless advice. I say useless – I'm sure you *should* take extra care while towing; I can't judge from experience because I've never towed anything. Should I ever do so, this road sign's advice is burned into my memory.

Perhaps Scotland is the towing-related accident capital of the world and this sign is part of a campaign to raise awareness. Awareness always needs raising. But they would attract a wider audience with 'Take extra care if you have noisy children in the back'. 'Take extra care while having a row with your partner.' And why stick to road-related stuff? Why doesn't the sign say 'Did you clean your teeth properly this morning?' Or how about 'When was the last time you talked to your mother? I mean *really* talked?' Or 'Don't make notes of what's on this sign for your *RT* column while driving'.

30 July–5 August

In vino veritas

Sparks fly when BBC presenters compare salaries

Tuesday night and I'm at the monthly meeting of the 1922 Committee – the secret gathering of BBC stars that gets its name from the fact no one is still sober by about 7.20 p.m. Even Fiona Bruce is slurring her words.

As I exclusively revealed in January, the meeting is open to anyone with an on-screen or on-air role at the BBC and there are only ever three items on the agenda.

1. Aren't we all terrific?
2. Aren't things going downhill but for our unstinting work?
3. Shouldn't we all be paid a good deal more just for being so marvellous?

This particular meeting is marked by bitter in-fighting over the BBC's decision to reveal that nineteen stars are paid more than five hundred thousand pounds a year, although at least no names are revealed. There is shock and outrage. A sense of disbelief on a scale I haven't witnessed since the night one female presenter offered Jeremy Paxman a personal demonstration of her vajazzle. I haven't been able to watch *BBC Breakfast* since.

'It's humiliating,' says one star. 'I can't believe they've put me in this awful position,' says another. 'Nice to Sir you, to Sir you nice,' says another, misjudging the mood of the evening.

The TV star who called it a humiliation is holding forth at

the bar, where former *EastEnder* Barbara Windsor has been forced to serve drinks despite her protests that 'I'm not in it any more'.

'I'll tell you why it's humiliating,' says the star. 'Without my name in the list of big earners, my friends and family think I might earn under half a million! The shame of it.' There is nodding all round, and once it stops the TV presenters offer to do more nodding as a cutaway.

Most anger is directed at those newspapers that have published guesstimates of what people earn. Is that a look of astonishment I see on Anne Robinson's face — I can't really tell — after she is placed underneath Alan Hansen? Chris Moyles and John Humphrys are in heated debate about the twenty-five grand that reportedly separates them. 'Don't you interrupt me.' 'Don't you interrupt *me*.' 'At least my name is in the title,' etc.

The volume in the room reaches levels that would wake the dead, or at least Trevor Eve, who is snoozing in the corner. Over the din I can hear another well-known voice bellow that a giant super-injunction should have been used to prevent coverage of any of this.

Finally, one presenter snaps. He stands on a table and begins to shout at the room. Out of habit, Barbara Windsor tells him to get out of her pub, until it's pointed out that she's not in it any more.

The man on the table's tirade silences the room. 'You stupid ******. Don't you see what these ***** are doing? They're trying to divide and rule! Those useless **** in management and on the BBC Trust are trying to set us against each other. Well, I for one say those ****, ******* and ***** will not succeed. I say we stand together, act as one and take them on. They're nothing without us. All for one and one for all.'

There is cheering at this rousing address and Eddie Mair is helped from the table and carried shoulder-high around the room, closing with the words 'Let's stop fighting among ourselves and blame the real enemy'. And, in unison, everyone in the room shouts 'Chiles and Bleakley!'

3–9 September

What lies within?

There's something nasty in the PM *fridge*

And now a true story from the office where broadcasting's finest talents make the Radio 4 shows *PM, The World at One, Broadcasting House, iPM, The World This Weekend, Today* and *The World Tonight*. The office where the finest Reithian traditions are passed from producers and editors of each generation, creating programmes that have become a cherished part of our society. I bring you an email sent last week to all staff in the department:

> Sorry to be the one to have to send this email, but I found another pair of socks in the fridge this evening. I put them next to the box of batteries. I am genuinely sorry if the person doing this has a medical condition. I'm not trying to be mean. Have you considered a coolbag? You can get them fairly cheap on Amazon [and there was a weblink here to a floral coolbag, £8.99]. But please stop putting your socks in the fridge. It's just plain gross. Thanks, Jastinder.

I suspect there are now a number of questions in your mind. Are there really medical conditions that are alleviated by chilled socks? Who in their right mind is going to touch those batteries? Who knew coolbags were so competitively priced? And, most pressingly, did someone really put socks in a fridge?

Jastinder used to work on *PM* and I know him to be a man of his word. He only left recently to join *The World Tonight* because we already had a producer called Jatinder and the confusion was driving everyone crazy.

'Jatinder, on line two it's the French Foreign Minister ready to do his recorded interview for *The World at One*.'

'Jastinder, on line one it's the Bavarian man who's trying to save Yvonne the cow, for *PM*.'

'Which line is it, Jastinder?'

'Sorry, Jatinder, I think it was two.'

'Did you say line one for me? I'll put it through to the studio.'

Luckily the French Foreign Minister was persuaded not to make a formal complaint after we offered him a box of vacuum-packed steaks.

All those programmes I mentioned (and a few more) really do share one fridge, so finding the sock culprit isn't going to be easy. What's more, we know people from other departments sometimes sneak in and use our fridge. I won't mention names because the lawyers have asked me not to. But if you take all the capital letters from the beginning of each sentence in this column and rearrange them, you'll have wasted your time because really the lawyers were very insistent.

I will keep you posted on the sock scandal. It's the worst thing to happen to the office fridge since the early days of Martha Kearney's interest in beekeeping, when she kept her bees in there, in the mistaken belief it would keep the honey fresher. I'll never forget the look on Robin Lustig's face when he innocently reached for his Müller Light only to be attacked by the swarm. He was picking wings out of his beard for weeks.

To eat, or not to eat

Can you help? I was about to enter a restaurant the other day when I spotted a sticker on the window saying 'Recommended by the *Good Food Guide*, 1997'. Should I have gone in?

10–16 September

My part in 9/11

When the going gets tough, the tough get . . .

'That's not an accident. That's terrorism.' It is 11 September 2001 and I'm speaking to the editor of *PM*, moments after the second plane hits the World Trade Center. It's not an especially insightful observation. Professor Paul Wilkinson I am not. Neither, sadly, is he. But at around the moment the White House chief-of-staff is whispering into the ear of the storyteller President Bush, at *PM* we realise this will be no ordinary day.

By six o'clock, at the end of an extended programme in which I perform in the mediocre-to-poor category, I'm eager to go home and sleep. The intensity of it all has been draining. It puts me in mind of royal obituary rehearsals, where we sit in studios for hours making pretend programmes to test our readiness for you-know-what.

I'm not sure I'm allowed to divulge more than that, except to say that executives always come up with creative ways of fictitiously seeing off senior royals. Don't get me wrong – we're not talking the opening scene of any episode of *Six Feet Under*, or *Dexter*. But I do get a pang of worry whenever Prince Philip goes carriage driving.

The odd thing about such rehearsals is that having lived a royal death for hours in the studio, it's odd to get in the car to drive home and find no mention of it on the news. It takes a moment to adjust.

Sadly, there's no such moment as I drive home that September day. Thousands of people are indeed dead, and the rest of us are glad to be alive. I celebrate by going to sleep at half past eight.

The phone rings shortly after. Work is urging me to go to Stansted Airport at once, where, it is rumoured, a special plane will fly a bunch of hacks to America so we can all win awards.

It's gone 11 p.m. and the only restaurant open is full of the cream of British broadcasting. Kate Adie is here. Jon Snow, too, I think. John Sergeant? A clutch of BBC TV reporters and radio producers, and every seat taken. There's some sniffiness at the remaining late-night offerings on the wipe-clean picture menu, but these people have all reported from the crappiest places in the world, so even the tomato salad holds no fear for them.

The place is awash with rumour about the plane. It seems laughable now, of course. US airspace was to be closed for days. But at the time we're hopeful of take-off before midnight. Then 0030. Then 0100. Then we hear the plane will fly to Canada and we'll all hire cars to drive to America. Pity the staff at the Avis desk in Toronto imagining British broadcasting's biggest stars elbowing each other out of the way in pursuit of the first vehicle out.

At 2 a.m. we're told to go home and come back at five, when the flight will probably leave. It doesn't. By morning even more journalists are here. Hours pass. Imagine the worst-delayed charter flight you've suffered and add fifty hacks all trying to outdo each other with hair-raising tales from their CVs.

Stansted's a busted flush but my producer and I get wind of a flight going from Heathrow. We leap in a car. After several fun hours at a crowded Heathrow we get wind of a flight from Gatwick. At Gatwick we . . .

I lost track in the end. We certainly visited four different airports that day. Stansted three times. And at 5 p.m., on one of the biggest news days of my life, I was not on air but on the M25, rushing to catch a plane that never left.

24–30 September

I made Doris Day cry

Radio regrets? This one still haunts me . . .

As I was saying to Lady Gaga the other day, you can't accuse me of name-dropping. So wild horses will not drag from me the identity of the former top BBC executive who identifies himself as president and sole member of the SMDDA – the Straight Men for Doris Day Association.

He is wetting himself over her new album. Actually, I don't think the album can be held solely responsible for that, which explains why he's a former top executive, but I digress.

Ms Day is back on the interview circuit. Michael Ball did

her for Radio 2. Sir Paul McCartney chatted to her for the *Daily Telegraph*. Ms Day's website reveals that Sir Paul graciously expressed interest in Day's forthcoming CD ... 'He's a very sweet man,' Ms Day said of McCartney. 'He's like me, very down to earth even though he's had so much success.'

Carmel Valley in California is where Ms Day calls home and I once made a brief pilgrimage to Carmel-by-the-Sea in the hope of bumping into her. Brief for several reasons. It turns out every old lady in a hat looks like Doris Day and they all quickly tired of my enquiries. The place is very dog-friendly and my allergies went crazy. Then there was my little romantic moment at midnight on the moonlit beach that was interrupted by the police, shining flashlights in my face, demanding to know what I was doing there alone.

I told them I was a friend of Doris's – they gave me a funny look as though they'd misheard – but I couldn't convince them, despite the fact that in the mid-nineties I had interviewed the great woman. More than that: I named a day after her.

On my 5 Live lunchtime show I'd been bemoaning how every illness, cause or product had time allocated to it, usually by bright PR companies. National Cough Week. Syrup is Fun Fortnight, that sort of thing. I declared that Friday of that week would be devoted to a silly idea suggested by a listener. And so National Doris Day was born.

Producers worked hard preparing half a dozen Doris-related items and one suggested we try to get an interview with her. We all laughed. Her reputation for reclusiveness was legendary. She made Howard Hughes look like he was doing the summer season on Blackpool North Pier.

But late on the Thursday afternoon the office rang, urging me to sober up and get back into work. Doris wanted to be interviewed. An hour later I was in the studio being put through to Doris Day. You might as well have put me through to God. I was ever so slightly nervous.

Her sunny voice broke the transatlantic phone hiss and we were off. She was delighted to hear of National Doris Day, and we chatted about her life and her dogs, who could be heard in the background. Five minutes passed. Ten. And I was still chatting to Doris Day. Then, after I asked something about her canine buddies, a break in her voice. I'll never forget her words: 'Oh, Eddie, I get all teary-eyed,' she said, as she sobbed quietly about her love of dogs.

I had made Doris Day cry.

When I reflect on the interview it doesn't please me that I moistened the tear ducts of a living legend. But then I think of what Doris and I have in common. Dogs make us both snuffle.

5–11 November

Of mice and men

Working in the PM *office is a scream*

It's not every day you hear a shriek from *The World Tonight*. The people who create the wiser older brother to *PM* sit just behind us at Television Centre. Unlike the *PM* team, they manage to get through the day without running around, noisily mocking each other and generally behaving like children.

Indeed, until last week's high-pitched scream, the only occasions to my knowledge that shrieking of any kind has happened at *The World Tonight* were when news broke of an impending change of government in Estonia, and the famous night the Argentine peso fell unexpectedly.

The scream didn't come from the programme's host, Robin Lustig. Robin Lustig is the doyen of radio news presenters. He's who I aspire to be if and when I grow up. Robin is professional to his fingertips and wouldn't scream if you set fire to him – goodness knows I've tried. He just calmly blows out my match, dampens down his smoky cuff and carries on recording his interview with the Prime Minister of Gambia. He's the sort of presenter who could go on the radio to intone that the world was about to end in a few minutes and you wouldn't feel so bad about it.

The scream came from one of the programme's producers, and on hearing it I swivelled round in my chair (the chiropractor says not to jerk my neck) to see her standing on her chair. She'd seen the office mouse. Humans are programmed to close their eyes when they sneeze, yawn if someone else in the room is yawning, and to jump on a chair if they see a mouse. Scientists believe we picked up the habit from *Tom and Jerry* cartoons and, sure enough, the producer in question, balanced precariously on a castored swiveller, kept yelling 'Thomas! Thomas!' in an accent that hinted at the American south.

I encountered the office mouse a while back, in the room where we hold our editorial meetings. Sitting on the floor (the chiropractor says not to sit on the chairs), I was suddenly aware of a small creature scurrying across the floor and over my shoes. My instinct was to leap on a chair, but you can imagine what the chiropractor feels about chair-leaping, so instead I let out a manly scream. Moments later our office first-aider arrived to attend to 'the girl who was being strangled'.

Now it seems there is more than one mouse in more than

one part of TV Centre. The newsroom above us on the first floor is particularly troubled and things are so bad there is a plan. It is, according to the email that went round, a 'three-pronged plan' and for me, the more prongs a plan has, the more I like it. Mice-proof bins, poison bait and electronic traps are being deployed, though the truth is if feckless hacks including me managed to squish all their lunches into their mouths instead of leaving half of it on the floor, we wouldn't be in this mess.

Longer term, the plan is to reduce the number of Television Centre mice by 20 per cent by 2016/17, with many of them being redeployed to Salford. My suggestion of inviting Les Dawson's mother-in-law for a visit was declined. ('I can always tell when the mother-in-law's coming to stay; the mice throw themselves on the traps.')

12–18 November

My flight into hell

Who knew I had so much emotional baggage?

'The airline would like to apologise for the delay with the bags and any inconvenience it may cause. The bags will take another thirty minutes. It's due to operational reasons.' I will return to that momentous sentence in a moment.

Modern airports are often described as giant shopping malls with landing strips. Wavy-roofed terminals are the home to thousands of retail opportunities and the odd check-in kiosk. No expense has been spared to ensure you are never more than twenty yards from a branch of WHSmith. Every square inch has been honed to maximise your potential retail value. Coffee, cake, caviar, watches, whisky and giant Toblerones are all to hand. Nothing is too much trouble. Who needs the high street? And at the end of it all you get to fly away somewhere!

Returning to the UK yesterday, I discovered a place at the airport that has missed the retail revolution of the past twenty years. I'm referring to the strange no-man's-land between passport control and customs. The baggage reclaim area.

A world away from the sparkling, shiny, customer-focused paradise that greets departing passengers, the baggage reclaim area is the land that time forgot. Low-ceilinged, dimly lit, windowless and quite possibly airless, it's the only part of the airport with no shops and only about ten seats.

I know what you're thinking . . . why should that matter? You go there, collect your bags and you're out. Who needs a coffee shop?

Well, I'm glad you raised that point. After waiting for twenty-five minutes, watching the bags from every other flight come and go, there was, at last, a tannoy announcement from the airline. The one at the start of the column. Please re-read it now.

As you can imagine, as I'd stood there for twenty-five min-utes, the news of a further thirty-minute delay was about as welcome as finding Piers Morgan next to you on your flight. I yearned for the woman on the tannoy to speak human: 'Look, we're really sorry about this – it's the last thing you want after a long flight. We've made a boo-boo, the man driving the luggage lorry fell asleep and what can I say? We're really sorry.' But no one is allowed to speak like that on tannoys. Her announcement entertained the possibility that some people wouldn't be inconvenienced by an hour-long wait for luggage. She could be oddly precise about the length of delay, but bafflingly vague on the cause. Operational reasons? Really? We'd never have guessed.

Further announcements followed after thirty minutes, promising the bags in ten minutes. Then another five. I made good use of the time. I checked for possible ways out. There were none. You're not allowed back up to passport control – they'll deport you. You can't go through customs without your bag – they'll shoot you. I had a very pleasant wander round the contours of all the baggage carousels, and back. I found one machine selling fizzy drinks and another selling chocolate. And I found ten people from our flight making full use of all the seating facilities.

The bags arrived an hour and a half after we landed. The woman in the Toblerone shop after customs agreed it was shocking and I asked why there wasn't at least a small coffee shop in the baggage hall. She thought it would be a good idea but was probably forbidden for operational reasons. And then I killed her.

19–25 November

Call me Blind Eddie

Thanks to my optician, I can barely see any more

Having successfully aged another year at the weekend, I thought this would be an appropriate moment to update you on a very personal topic first addressed here last August: my steady decline into decrepitude.

You will recall (unless your memory is like mine) that I had detected some blurriness in the printed word. Reading close up was becoming weirdly difficult. It wasn't a one-off, so I was able to discount the usual causes of such reading problems: darkness, tiredness and drunkenness.

The British Printing Industries Federation wouldn't return my call, so in the end I took the unusual step of having my eyes tested. The optician was mildly surprised that this was my first eye test since I was at school (don't worry, I helped her back into her chair), and after a whirlwind of charts, puffs of air and flashes of light, we established that I would need reading glasses.

I took this shocking news as I take all shocking news ('They're making *The World at One* even longer') – that is to say, in my stride. Glasses were duly chosen (I look like Jim Bowen) and helpful advice was doled out by speccy colleagues. One said to use them whenever possible in order to train my eyes. Another cautioned that I should do the opposite – that constant use of the glasses would make me reliant on them. I should use them only when I really struggled to read.

Here I am a year later and I can't read anything without glasses. Twelve months ago my naked eyes could confidently examine the ingredients list on supermarket items (why do they persist in calling sugar fructose?); they could read texts from my agent (how did she get this number?); even the small print on my Radio 4 contract (I must not use the word 'runt' on air). Now my arms aren't long enough to do any of that unaided and so, at the age of forty-six, if I leave the house without my specs I'm unable to read anything.

My colleague who advised against constant use of the glasses adheres to a sort of opticians' conspiracy theory. They're like drug dealers, she says. She believes opticians like to get us hooked on their high-priced products with their pleasing reassurances that they'll just be for reading, safe in the knowledge that within a year we'll be back demanding more expensive and stronger glasses that we need all the time – just to function and get through the day. Apparently, quite a lot of people at my time of life believe this. Opticians, I am told, reckon it's a load of old cobblers put about by people struggling to cope with the effects of ageing. What do you think?

Coming soon: my trip to get my hearing tested.

Nothing to say about Jimmy Savile

A footnote to all the coverage of Sir Jimmy's recent death. When news of his passing reached the *PM* office that Saturday afternoon, producers began to telephone people who knew him or worked with him, in the hope they would appear on the programme to pay tribute. I am told that one very famous disc jockey – whose name is as well-known as Sir Jimmy's – was called and asked to appear but he said to the producer, with admirable candour: 'Do you know what? I don't think I could think of a single nice thing to say about him,' and hung up.

26 November–2 December

Brucie knows best . . .

Only the dead take early retirement

They used to say that the BBC staff pension was so generous because it never had to pay out for very long, although that was back in the day when all pension funds had money. Having toiled all their lives for the Corporation, people would open their 'You're Retiring!' card full of good wishes and abuse from colleagues, make a speech about how BBC morale has never been so low, and within six weeks they'd be dead. Very sad, especially for the wags who'd written 'Hey, you'll be dead within six weeks!' in the card.

My favourite sequence of radio programmes was on Sunday mornings on Radio 4. I would lie in bed listening to a beautifully written ten-minute news bulletin at nine o'clock, which always seemed to be read by Brian Perkins, followed by a five-minute newspaper review with Brian Perkins and then, at 9.15, *Letter from America*, which always seemed to be presented by Alistair Cooke. When that finished at half past it would be time to slither out of bed and face the day. It was a wonderful routine that I'm sure millions of people enjoyed as I did, until *Broadcasting House* came along. Schedule-ruining barbarians.

Mr Cooke – and don't you wish you could hear his thoughts on the current US presidential race – stopped sending his letters early in March 2004. By the end of the month he was dead.

Last month a man who was more famous in America than Alistair Cooke was in the UK stopped presenting his weekly despatches on the CBS television network. Andy Rooney had popped up at the end of the highly rated current affairs programme *60 Minutes* to deliver a personal essay more than a thousand times.

Between 1978 and October 2011 Mr Rooney – who was half-man, half-eyebrows – would speak straight to camera for two or three minutes about anything that took his fancy. Modern manners, road maps, politicians . . . it didn't matter, and he became an icon, not least because there was no one left on television anywhere on the planet who was allowed to just speak directly to the viewer for three minutes without the 'help' of graphics, music or a panel of guests.

When CBS announced that, at the age of ninety-two, there would be no more weekly appearances for *A Few Minutes with Andy Rooney* it was headline news across America. But the door was left open. The network made it clear that Mr Rooney would 'always have the ability to speak his mind on *60 Minutes* when the urge hits him'. But I remember thinking at the time, Poor Andy, he'll be dead within six weeks. And, sure enough, on 4 November he was.

The lesson here, particularly perhaps for broadcasters, is never to give up work. Sir Bruce Forsyth is aware of this. The day after Mr Rooney died, Sir Brucie was fronting the Bonfire Night edition of *Strictly* when he revealed that he'd refused requests to personally light fireworks because the instructions said you should light the blue touch-paper and retire.

So my advice: don't retire. Everyone who does ends up dead. And, in the same vein, if someone comes up to you and shouts in your ear that you've just become Britain's oldest living person, punch their lights out. That title is fatal.

3–9 December

Just a moment

Nicholas Parsons is a hero for our age

The world is divided into people who love *I'm Sorry I Haven't a Clue* but loathe *Just a Minute* and vice versa. I've watched heated arguments between both sides. 'What's funny about singing some words to the tune of another?' Or, 'Speaking for sixty seconds – what's funny about that?' You can't get them to see the other person's point of view. It's like TV viewers arguing about *The X Factor* and *Strictly*, or Conservatives arguing about Europe.

I like both shows. It's impossible to dislike anything with Barry Cryer in it, and *Just a Minute* is always entertaining. Frustratingly, I'm not usually around for its live broadcast, and it's still bafflingly impossible to download and keep radio programmes on the iPlayer. Neither is *Just a Minute* available as a podcast. The alphabetical list of available Radio 4 podcasts goes from *In Touch* to *Last Word* (in touch to out of touch?) without an intervention by the letter J, although I'm sure there is a good explanation for this.

And so I've found myself in recent weeks buying old episodes online and downloading them to my MP3 player. I would have thought it impossible for previous panellists to top the wit and erudition of Paul Merton and the much-missed Clement Freud, but I've been roaring with laughter at Peter Jones, Wendy Richard, Derek Nimmo, Linda Smith and of course Kenneth Williams. Why couldn't they just go on entertaining us for ever?

As I write I'm halfway through the *Just a Minute* thirty-fifth anniversary special. Clement Freud has been bickering with Sheila Hancock, and Graham Norton got the topic of 'suspenders' and revealed a lack of detailed knowledge about where on a woman's body they go.

The man who holds the show together is Nicholas Parsons. Incessantly mocked and challenged in every edition, he is the unsung hero of proceedings. He's appeared in every programme since *Just a Minute* began and earlier this month he appeared live on *PM* to talk about the forthcoming forty-fifth anniversary celebrations, which include two shows being recorded in India, and a short run of TV editions being recorded last month for BBC2. But the great man almost didn't appear.

We'd set aside seven minutes and sent a radio car to Nicholas's house. But with moments to go there was increasing anxiety in our studio. We had nothing else to go to and were relying on Nicholas and the radio car meeting, as arranged, outside Nicholas's front door. The radio car man told us he was through the main gates but was still looking for Nicholas. I imagine he lives in something like Downton.

With the penultimate item on *PM* about to finish, and with seven minutes of dead air looming, our producer tried to get through to Nicholas on his mobile, so we could at least do the interview over the phone. But Nicholas was on his phone, trying to guide the radio car to his front door.

With ten seconds to spare, we got through and Nicholas was magnificent. Which is just as well, as I couldn't have filled seven minutes without a lot of hesitation, deviation and repetition.

10–16 December

Big head strikes again

My huge cranium is now preserved for posterity

Recently, I felt a bit like the Queen. This doesn't happen often. If ever I find myself talking to a camera in front of a well-dressed Christmas tree, or slamming a bottle of champers onto the side of a newly minted vessel, I do feel as one with the monarch. But in all candour, neither of those things has ever happened, so they don't count.

Last Sunday, however, I did feel a little like the Queen,

albeit without her nice line in tweedy skirts and winning ways with cheery small talk.

A colleague asked if I would do a sitting for him, as a live model. Stop tittering.

He wanted to make my head out of clay. My first response, of course, was to point out that my head is already full of clay, or at least that's how it feels most days. My second was to warn of a surge in the global price of clay as I have rather an enormous head. It's visible from space, like the Great Wall of China and Nancy Dell'Olio's embarrassment. For him to buy enough clay to represent my oversized noggin would lead to a clay futures frenzy.

He assured me that he could complete the project with perhaps as little as a ton of clay. Two if he did my neck. And so I came to be sitting on a swivel chair in the middle of his south London front room, while a few feet away my besmocked work colleague demonstrated that he was as adept at forming clay head lines as he is at writing news headlines.

All I had to do was sit perfectly still for two hours. Occasionally I would swivel in the chair to afford him a scintillating view of my left ear, then my right ear, then the glorious back of my head.

Early in the session the Queen popped into my head. She must have done sittings for scores of artists during her reign, usually Rolf Harris. She must have to sit there for hours at Sandringham or at Buckingham Palace while nervous artists scurry around, assuring her that it's all looking terrific. As I sat, I began to channel the Queen.

'Have you come far?' I heard myself saying. 'Why did no one see this economic crisis coming?' and 'A happy Christmas to you all.'

Most of the time, though, I just sat quietly. I rather enjoyed the experience of sitting down and not doing anything. No reading, fiddling with the TV remote or making rude shadow puppets. Just sitting quietly. How often do we do that, do you think? I've never meditated but if it's half as relaxing as sitting staring out the window/looking at the fireplace/the back wall/the back of my own clay head, then I am going to take it up. I imagine Her Majesty rather enjoys her sittings for the same reason. And she probably knows Rolf well enough by now to tell him to pipe down if he's becoming uber-chatty.

I have a few more sessions to go. By the end of the first sitting the clay representation of my head put me in mind of a Neanderthal, so I think he's on to something.

Mouse update

One of our office mice scurried across the floor in front of me last Friday, having emerged from desks at *The World Tonight*. He seemed fine, unlike some of his friends and family, eight of whom, I'm told, are no more.

2012

My walk of shame

How Kermit and Co. left me with a bruised ego

I learnt a little something about myself last weekend and it wasn't pretty. In fact it was uglier than 'Come as Olive from *On the Buses*' night down at the Drag and Drop.

A little background first. The *PM* editor loves the Muppets. Seriously loves them, and not just because, as she always says, 'I work with a bunch of Muppets' (drum, cymbal). She's had a lifelong adoration. If I tell you that it was she who invited Kermit the Frog to address the Oxford Union, you'll have some idea. The day Jim Henson died was the same day my editor-to-be was due to sit her history GCSE. Her mother hid all the newspapers so as not to put her off.

Jo is a gifted, brilliant editor (happy with that, Legal Dept?) but the constant Muppets referencing can get wearing, especially when it's in our editorial meetings. Everything that happens is like something that happened in *The Muppet Show* (or their films). The euro crisis 'reminds me of that scene in *The Muppets Take Manhattan* when Kermit . . . ' The US presidential election 'reminds me of that scene in *The Great Muppet*

Caper when Kermit . . . ' and Antony Worrall Thompson 'reminds me of Animal . . . '

When it emerged last year that a brand-new Muppet movie was coming out, we agreed that we'd go to the first showing. I know what you're thinking – what a suck-up. Going to the movies with your *boss*? And you're right, of course. I do it all the time to try to curry favour.

I calculated that sitting in a cinema was less degrading than the time I pricked sausages for an hour at the Radio 4 controller's barbecue, or my foray into making balloon animals for the kids at Mark Thompson's last cheese and wine. I still maintain that, from all but one angle, those balloons resembled an inquisitive tortoise.

Kermit and Co. were the subject of an email my editor received a few weeks ago, offering two tickets for a special showing of *The Muppets*. She was extremely excited about the prospect of seeing the film so soon. I was excited about being invited into that exclusive club inhabited only by the likes of Barry Norman and Andrew Collins. I've heard that film critics get invited to swish screenings, where they lounge in vast luxurious reclining seats while being served champagne and stuffing as many delicious canapés as possible into their mouths. And they get to see a film.

I was about to be part of that club. There was probably a special entrance to that exclusive bit of the cinema. Probably with two or three feet of red rope strung between gold-plated stands, and possibly a doorman to keep away the ordinary folk who, unlike me, were not great film critics.

Last Sunday, as I arrived in Leicester Square in search of the VIP entrance, I was appalled to see a HUGE queue of non-film critics snaking for miles. Naturally, I marched to the head of the line and asked where I could find the special screening of *The Muppets*. The doorman said I was in the right place and was welcome to join the queue half a mile away.

The walk to the end of the line would have been less humiliating had I been wearing Fozzie's fart shoes. The film? **** My ego? *****

11–17 February

My private passion

I'm outing myself as a country music fan

It will come as no surprise to people who know me – but it might startle the uninitiated to learn – that there's nothing I like more than Willie. And Alan. And Dolly. Mr Nelson, Mr Jackson and, of course, Ms Parton are among the biggest stars of country music and I count myself as a fan. It's a genre that never fails to arouse strong feelings among enthusiasts and detractors. To give you some indication, opinion polls suggest that people who passionately hate or love country are utterly indifferent to Marmite.

Like most folks, I believe that what people listen to in the privacy of their own earphones is entirely up to them. I've not made a secret of my love of country but, equally, never go to work in a brightly coloured Stetson, sheriff's badge and chaps. You have to keep some stuff for the weekend.

But last Friday I found myself in Glasgow, preparing a forthcoming Radio 4 special entitled *Eddie Goes Country*. I'm hoping that, if it meets with a favourable reaction, there will be spin-off series. I envisage a six-parter in which I confront everyday situations that frighten me (*Eddie Goes Clammy*); I meet posh people (*Eddie Goes Classy*); I take illegal drugs to measure their effect (*Eddie Goes Class A*); and an uproarious follow-up to *Eddie Goes Country* in which I'm vile to all around me, behaving appallingly, though I can't for the life of me think of a title for it.

The country programme tries to establish whether my affinity for the music runs deeper than I imagine (SPOILER ALERT: it does). I got to meet Ricky Ross (check his excellent show *Another Country* on BBC iPlayer) and I dropped by the Celtic Connections festival to catch up with the likes of Eleanor McEvoy and Dick Gaughan. They were terrific and gave us great material.

Best of all, I got to linger backstage in the afternoon during sound checks. Never done that before, and while everyone else was nonchalantly tweaking knobs and routinely plucking guitars, I was unspeakably excited with the sheer show-businessness of it all. It was *Eddie Goes Crazy*.

For the performers, the preparation was a necessary part of their weekly routine. For me, it was thrilling to hear them say, 'I'm a bit bassy-trebley', 'Can you worble the grotblaster up two notches?' and other things I didn't understand.

When one star came backstage having finished his preparations, we caught up over one of those silver coffee containers with the squirty button. Eager to learn some country/showbiz secrets, I asked him what he'd be doing between now and the big performance in the evening. He said they were planning a bite to eat at around six.

Me: 'But what about until then? What do you plan to do for the rest of the afternoon?'

Star: 'Chain smoke.'

Beeb boss on the edge

Went to see *Man on a Ledge* last week – the British remake. It stars Mark Thompson as a man who's just sitting, staring out the window, minding his own business, when Lord Patten bursts in and forces him out onto the narrow ledge but tries to persuade everyone it was Thompson's idea alone to do so. Thought the plot was a bit far-fetched.

18–24 February

One giant leap year

Plan something extraordinary for 29 February

Calendars can be funny things. It's been the Chinese Year of the Dragon for weeks now, but I'm *still* writing Year of the Rabbit on cheques. That joke is probably older than the Gregorian calendar – and about as funny. But, as the old Chinese proverb says: 'A doctor who understands time is a wise man; a wise man who controls time is Doctor Who'.

I'd like to apologise for the slightly surreal opening to this week's column. I've been imbibing a herbal tea concoction recommended by a knowledgeable-sounding woman working out of a densely stocked micro-shop in Chinatown and, if I have too much of it at once, I don't know what day of the week it is.

Luckily, those Gregorians, from the long-lost land of Gregoria, anticipated this and charted each day of the year in a regular pattern. If you know what day it was yesterday, it's possible to discover which day of the week it is today. This has been the case for hundreds of years and it's a brilliantly simple notion – enhanced in modern times by calendars, both official and unofficial, bearing the likeness of Sir Cliff Richard and the stars of *Hollyoaks*.

Unlike Sir Cliff, a wrinkle is added occasionally. A day is tacked to the end of February, throwing everyone out of kilter. The month's usual symmetrical simplicity with its 4x7 configuration is askew. Like a prospective Parliamentary candidate, 29 February pays us a visit once every four years. It stops the Earth from tilting too far back on its axis, scientists tell us, and as such we should be grateful. But it causes myriad problems.

Famously in 2000 – Y2K, if you will – the world's computers almost ground to a halt when it was realised that scientists, preoccupied with fixing the Y2K bug, had forgotten to add a 29 February. By the time they realised on 2 January, all the calendars were on people's walls and it was too embarrassing to have a big recall.

Even more embarrassing is the number of people who appear for all the world to be in their forties, fifties and sixties, but can honestly tell people they've had only twelve or so birthdays, thanks to them being born on 29 February. Is this a victory in the battle against ageism? I'm writing a letter to a newspaper.

Sorry. I had some more tea. The point is we're coming up to an unusual, not to say special point in our calendar. 29 February is like a free day – an extra day. And that's why, this year on *PM*, we're asking listeners to do something unusual to mark the occasion, and since you've gone to the trouble of reading this far, can I invite you as a *Radio Times* reader to do the same?

Perhaps you could pick up the phone and actually speak to that person with whom you only ever exchange Christmas cards. Or file those CDs in alphabetical order. Start learning that language. Take out that *Radio Times* subscription. Sorry, I had some more tea again.

Once you've decided on your idea, on the day itself find some way to record your thing. Write it down, video it. And together we'll make this the most special 29 February in history! I hear stirring music. I see bright lights. What the hell is in this tea?

(Passes out . . .)

Pesto says sorry

BBC business editor sees sense and ends our feud

For weeks on *PM*, I have been urging listeners to take a leap on 29 February. It's a day that comes round only once every four years – an extra day in our lives. So why not use it as cover for doing something different? If it all goes disastrously wrong, we can blame it on the weird extra day and return to our lives as normal on 1 March.

All sorts of listeners are planning to seize the extra day, or *carpe extra diem* as I believe the phrase goes. One woman in her sixties will be getting her first tattoo. A man will compose a piece of classical music. Another woman will pick up her hula-hoop after a gap of more than fifty years. Someone else is taking the day off to listen to unheard recordings made by his nan. A man called Rupert said he would launch a new paper on the 29th, but it turns out it's the wrong day of the week for him.

What do you plan to do? And what about me? I was inspired by the listeners who told us they plan to patch up broken relationships. A nightclub bouncer intends to write to his estranged brother. A woman will contact a relative to try to heal a rift. It's so easy in life for a cross word here or a threatening letter from a lawyer there to become a feud, the cause of which no one can remember.

That's why I invited the BBC's business editor, Robert Peston, to co-present *PM* with me, live, for the entire hour, on Wednesday 29 February. It's high time we both grew up and got over the bitter and angry feud that Robert alone caused. When people tune in on Wednesday they will hear my 29 February philosophy put into action, as I share the *PM* studio and the presentation job with Mr Peston.

It'll be quite an occasion and to whet your appetite Robert has kindly agreed to write the next few words of this column to demonstrate our joint determination to end our angry feud. Here's the keyboard, Robert . . .

Hello. This is Robert, and thank you Eddie for your magnificently magnanimous gesture. Of course, everyone knows the feud was not your fault. How could a man who does such tireless – and unsung – charity work ever have a bad thought in his head? I take full responsibility and will be honoured to be at your side during the special edition of PM *on Wednesday. I'm getting a little bit emotional now – just a manly misting – but I can barely make out the numbers on this Bank of England forecast in front of me. Not that it matters. I'll hand you back to Eddie now, you handsome devil.*

Thank you, Robert. My laptop hasn't been this tear-stained since I caught up with the midwife thing on the iPlayer.

I'm not sure how *PM* will sound with *two* presenters . . . what sort of madness is that? Still, if Robert and I can publicly heal the rift that he has kindly acknowledged in writing was all his fault, then some good will come of it. So please join us on Wednesday, for the special programme entitled *Eddie Mair's PM with Me Eddie Mair (and Robert Pesto).*

17–23 March

I name this building

The Mair Extension? It's only a matter of time . . .

How delightful to read the director-general's email to BBC staff recently, announcing that the Egton Wing, part of the new Broadcasting House, is to be renamed the Peel Wing. It is on the site of Egton House, which was the home of Radio 1, from where John Peel broadcast throughout his career.

As Mark Thompson put it, 'John's death in 2004 was sudden and shocking, especially for those of us who had grown up with him. However, his legacy lives on today not just in the UK, but around the world. He was a great ambassador for the BBC, and as we move into the BBC's iconic new home at Broadcasting House, the Peel Wing will be a fitting tribute to a man who personified so much of what the BBC stands for – quality, creativity and innovation.'

If you're like me – and I hope for your sake you're not – several things will be racing through your mind right now. First, what a good idea it is. Second, how did I get permission to quote from an internal director-general email? And third, which other broadcasters deserve the honour of having buildings named after them . . . perhaps those with a column in *Radio Times*? I'll give you a moment to locate the person I'm thinking of.

The truth is, I didn't get permission to quote from an internal BBC email. Call me irresponsible. Call me cavalier. Call me Susan. The point is, most BBC hacks who get internal BBC emails into the public domain never get permission. They do so by leaking the contents to friends on the newspapers. At least I'm upfront about it. Now I've started, it feels quite liberating. I'm going to quote from more emails Mark Thompson has sent me personally. Yes I am. Look, here are some highlights from his most recent correspondence: 'over-paid gob on a stick', 'worse than Peston' and 'so help me I will come down to the *PM* office and personally bite you'. He has a lovely sense of humour.

As for other individuals who might deserve, in the fullness of time, to have some corner of the BBC named after them: let's honour a former Radio 1 colleague of John Peel by creating Noel's Broadcasting House Party. The Nigel Pargetter Roof Garden. And I would have thought the studios where they make *EastEnders* could accommodate an Anna Wing Wing.

One can't help hoping that some day the broadcasters of the future might be creating radio magic within the confines of the Eddie Mair Extension. I like to imagine that long after I'm dead, people will climb the Mair Stairs, speak into the Mair Mikes and leave work through Eddie Mair's front entrance.

Robert Peston: an appreciation

Robert and I have been pretty hard to avoid in recent times. We co-presented an edition of *PM* on Leap Day, 29 February. A couple of weeks ago we popped up in *Radio Times* in photographs that appeared to show us in the same room together, though in truth it was all done with Photoshop.

The editor has asked that I say a few kind words about Robert, but as you can see I'm completely out of room.

21–27 April

Morning pop-pickers

Confessions from my days on the breakfast show

It was heartening to read that former Radio 1 DJs Mike Read, Tony Blackburn and Dave Lee Travis ('collective age of two hundred') are together again playing hits from the sixties, seventies and eighties on the Magic Radio network. Schedule your listening properly by adding Radio 1 vets Simon Bates on Smooth Radio and Steve Wright (great show, Steve) on Radio 2 and you may never have to live in the present day at all. Finally, radio listening to suit my wardrobe.

There is, of course, a double standard here. Retired Radio 1 stars will always find a home on other stations because listeners love wallowing in musical memories. But what about presenters who've made their name in news? What happens to the current crop of Radio 4 voices (collective age 984) when their programmes are refreshed? Will there be an outlet for the octogenarian Robin Lustig? 'There was trouble in Liberia and the President of Uzbekistan faced a crisis in Parliament – but what's the year?' Will ninety-five-year-old Martha Kearney be ensconced at some community station somewhere, announcing, 'The world at ... wait, what time is it?'

Blackburn told the *Daily Mail* that the trio's shows were different from other 'classic music' programmes because they didn't use playlists. 'We pick our own music. It's not about audience research or focus groups – it's about gut reaction.'

I would always prefer Tony Blackburn to choose the music over a market-research wonk or a computer. But, personally,

I've never been able to tell the difference between a station with a human playlist and a station run by robots.

But what do I know? Here's how I treated the listener back in the days (here we go) when I hosted the breakfast show on Radio Tay: 05.30–09.00, Monday to Friday, a cheerful mix of music, news, quizzes and blah, blah, blah. This was the mid-eighties, when a computer could no more have chosen and played music than been used in cars to guide you to your destination. We had an alphabetised record library with seven-inch discs, two players in the studio and a woman whose job it was to listen to each new release, time it, time its intro and put a label on it bearing all this information, plus whether or not it faded at the end. How we survived, I'll never know. They didn't introduce studio clocks until 1987.

My initial Blackburn-like enthusiasm for enthralling listeners with carefully chosen tracks began to wear off after a few months of getting up at 3.30 a.m. But I developed a system to bypass the station's music policy. All presenters had to play music from the A and B playlists – current hits that were kept in the studio. But every third record had to be an individual choice. My genius idea? Don't spend hours searching for records to play, just grab a bunch from one shelf and slip them into the show. No more time wasted and no one will ever notice.

The system was a time-saving treat, affording me an extra half-hour in bed each morning. Until the Head of Music sidled up to me one morning as I dashed out the door at 09.01. 'So, Eddie, it was R today, was it?'

I stopped my system immediately and dreamt of the day computers could choose music for us.

28 April–4 May

It could be you

Fancy being boss of the Beeb? Get in quick!

And so the moment has come for all those whiners who believe they could do a much better job than Mark Thompson to put up or shut up. Or at least shut up until his successor is appointed and then begin moaning about them.

The job specification for BBC director-general has been published. We all have until 7 May to submit our applications. To be precise, we have until 11.59 p.m. on that date, and the ad is quite specific: 'no late applications will be accepted', so don't even THINK about waiting until there's half an hour to go, then trying to hail a taxi in the rain, before running in the style of the young Norman Wisdom into the revolving doors of Television Centre, clutching your damp application and demanding to be included. They'll take a very dim view of that, if my experience from the last time round is anything to go by.

There are a number of things that strike me about the full job description, which I have been through with a fine-tooth comb (finally, a use for it). The specification is emphatic that the 'role will be based in central London', which is fair enough. It's not as though the Corporation is involved in any kind of push to get out of London. There's talk that some day plans may be drawn up for a broadcasting centre in Salford, but unless that gets off the drawing board, central London it must be.

I especially enjoy the bit that says the next D-G will show that he/she can 'thrive under legitimate and constant public and political scrutiny'. I imagine the meeting at which that wording was agreed . . . 'Tiffany, what's the best way of saying that whichever loser gets this job is going to become a hate figure for all the BBC-despisers in the press who will not rest until the entire organisation is either a profitable subsidiary of their own media empires or shut down entirely?'

'I don't know, Tarquin, but we also have to find a way of conveying that some MPs think that bias is asking critical questions two days in a row and will be on the phone every five minutes demanding that they get their way while hinting darkly that the licence fee could be on its way out.'

I have carefully considered my position on the director-generalship. At first I thought it would be wrong to endorse an individual publicly. After all, a yes from me on this would be like a yes from Simon Cowell. It would propel my chosen candidate into a probably unassailable position and render the others destitute. I couldn't do that to them or their families.

Then I thought, to hell with that. I want Baroness Neville-Jones to get the job. You may be wondering why I am endorsing a name that has not so far come up in all the speculation. Well, it could be because the Baroness is a respected member of the political establishment, who has a proven track record in diplomacy, negotiation and intelligence. It could be because she has been a BBC governor, or that she has the communication skills a D-G needs.

All of that is true. But the main reason I am suggesting the good Baroness is that I drew her name in the *PM* office sweepstake and stand to make thirty pounds. Please spread the word.

12–18 May

Soldiering on . . .

A cough won't stop this dedicated broadcaster

I don't normally bother you with my health problems. That's why I silently soldiered on through the Paper Cut of October '09 and the Possible Wax Build-Up of March '11. During both traumas I did not sully the reading or listening public with my personal difficulties.

When journalism's historians come to laud my contribution, long after I am dead, they will pay tribute to a titan of the profession, who never let his own crises stand in the way of his unswerving commitment to first-class, well-researched, intelligent journalism. Like that man on the Scott expedition who went off. You know, into the snow . . . may be some time etc. Him.

I have always gritted my teeth and stiffened my upper lip, even during my Dental/Philtrum Catastrophe of November '11. But I cannot stay silent any longer. All winter, colleagues have been coming into the *PM* office with coughs, sneezes and related diseases. I have managed to avoid picking up their bugs through adherence to strict hygiene rules ('Stay away from me, you loser') and my patented Stay Healthy Bug-Killing Regimen (three brandies a night). Despite all those efforts, I'm afraid I must reveal to you a health problem that threatens to overwhelm me.

I have a slight cough.

I've felt it approaching menacingly for days now, like the *Mastermind* theme, or a breakfast meeting with the Radio 4 controller. A hint of a chill and a slight feeling of dread (I'm talking about my cough again here) were the harbingers of a restless night last night. I woke around 2 a.m. with a feeling of constriction on my throat I haven't experienced since my last breakfast meeting. The pain was like nothing any human being had ever experienced or ever would. Like giving birth to a large child in my larynx. Happily it subsided after I took one pain-relief tablet.

This morning, though, there is a vicious, explosive cough, and more than a little mucus on my keyboard. Plus my voice has dropped two octaves. How can I convey how deep my voice suddenly is? Try to imagine Orson Welles after a really big night out, followed by an hour of heavy cigar-smoking and gargling with razor blades. Or just think of Bea Arthur.

Broadcasting in these conditions is tricky. If there are long periods when the microphone is live, it's impossible for your cough not to be heard. Efforts at muzzling the sound can make things worse. Charlotte Green can be enunciating perfectly the latest crisis to befall an obscure foreign dictator while I cover my nose and mouth at the precise climax of my cough, to produce an unexplained sound akin to a buffalo farting in a muddy bath. It's not good radio.

But of course I must go in. I mean, how could the nation carry on if it doesn't get its news from me … even a heavily congested and befuddled me? No. I will go to work, for the public good.

Did I mention I am freelance?

Lovely doors

Amid all the coverage of the Culture Secretary Jeremy Hunt (not a name to broadcast when befuddled) this vignette from my editor, who watched all the coverage of him arriving home and leaving for his incessant jogging: 'He's got a lovely front door.'

9–15 June

Killer Queen

Is the National Anthem musical bleach?

Can the Queen kill Keane? I hope so. I realise that's an unkind thought at any time – especially in this Jubilee-est of weeks. The thing is, I am desperate.

If you know Keane's music at all, you'll know that besides the soulful lyrics and the incredible sound of Tom Chaplin's voice, they have a way with soaring, catchy melodies that makes Stock Aitken Waterman sound like Philip Glass. Downloading their latest album was an enormous mistake. For the past fortnight I've woken up with one of their songs going round in my head. This morning it was 'The Starting Line'. Yesterday it was 'Silenced by the Night'. This is happening despite the fact I've made a point of not listening to the album for some time.

I am going to have to resort to a suggestion sent to *PM* by a listener, after an item we did on earworms. She suggested getting 'God Save the Queen' into your head as it kills any earworm . . . 'musical bleach' she called it. I'll give it a go and let you know.

Silence is golden

Whenever I'm asked to give advice to people starting out in journalism or broadcasting, I'm afraid my mind goes completely blank, aside from a Keane track. I got into radio thanks to a lot of luck and some persistence, but try telling that to a bright-eyed teenager hanging on your every word and you'll be met with a look of bitter disappointment. I usually try to remedy things by stumbling through the worst kind of advice clichés: work hard, apply yourself, be prompt, never work with Corrie Corfield . . . advice that doesn't sparkle with originality but is undeniably correct.

Luck probably plays more of a part in our careers than anything, though again that doesn't really help earnest youngsters looking for job tips. They don't want to hear that success is like a lottery scratchcard only with fewer grey bits of rubbed-off card on the floor.

Here's an example. Last month, *PM* won a Sony Gold Award for best breaking-news coverage, for the night President Mubarak was toppled in Egypt. There *was* a lot of hard work involved, not least from the editor that night, Fiona Leach, and Hugh Sykes, who has never sounded better, reporting live from Tahrir Square.

We opened the programme by broadcasting, without commentary, the sounds of cheering from the square. It was far more effective than any words I could have said, or clips of politicians we could have played. About twenty minutes later we did the same thing again, broadcasting just the live cheering for what seemed like ages. The Sony judges in their citation said the programme's 'arresting use of sound took the listener to the heart of the action . . . great radio made by people who understand great radio'.

Very nice of them. What we haven't admitted until now is that, while the sound-rich opening of the programme was a piece of sound editorial judgement, the return to the square was because we had completely run out of stuff. Phone lines down. No guests. Nothing to go to but dead air. Bad luck.

So I said something to the effect of 'Let's cross live again to hear history in the making'. It bought us some time and, it seems, an award. Good luck.

Breaking news

I now have the National Anthem stuck in my head.

7–13 July

Brideshead visited

I'm catching up on the tale of Sebastian's teddy

Jeremy Vine apparently checked his *Newsnight* viewing figures every morning. *Every* morning. I have *begged* Jeremy to write a book about this sort of thing.

In telly, the overnight audience statistics give an almost instant daily readout of how many people watched, how old they were, which social class they belong to and which genitals they have.

In radio, we get those figures once every three months. We aren't slaves to the 'overnights'. I like to think this makes us true public service broadcasters, guided not by the travails of our market share and naked popularity, but by our Reithian principles. It's like a calling.

But as you know I'm full of crap. The truth is, if radio could afford to have overnight statistics, we'd be studying them more closely than a tax inspector going through Jimmy Carr's receipts. Did our ten-minute discussion on the euro cause a switch-off at 17.10? Was there a spike in listeners for our talking goat item at 17.53? I don't doubt that we would tailor our programmes to suit what we thought the figures were telling us.

Thankfully, it's unlikely to happen, not least because in TV the hegemony of the overnights is waning. The Personal Video Recorder, with its time-shifting magic, means programme-makers can no longer judge the success of their ventures on the snapshot of the overnights. Sky's Director of Spending Money, Stuart Murphy, told the *Guardian* recently: 'It's disingenuous to say we don't look at all at overnights ... But it feels a bit thick. It's like judging someone on the first date and not whether it's been a three-year success.'

One of the shows Stuart airs on Sky Atlantic is *Smash*, a new musical drama that, when it aired on NBC, had overnight figures so low they were mistaken for Piers Morgan's. But America's PVRs were whirring, particularly those belonging to people aged eighteen to forty-nine, whom advertisers love. The flop in the overnights has been given a second series. The *New York Times* declared that *Smash* had been 'saved by delayed viewership'.

The other week *Radio Times* rang to enquire about my viewing and listening habits. I couldn't think of anything outside news and current affairs that I watch 'live'. Now we can stream or download TV from the recent past or ancient history, I'm caught in my own telly timewarp. Thank goodness I have the wardrobe to match.

I watched the first three seasons of *Breaking Bad* in quick succession. Yesterday I caught the first two episodes of *House*, dating from 2004; and they only stopped making *House* this year. I've also taken to watching, for the first time, *Brideshead Revisited*. All of this viewed by means other than conventional television. How will they count my viewership?

It makes office talk about last night's telly viewing redundant. 'Did you catch *EastEnders*?'

'No, but I'm wondering whether Sebastian's teddy is going to survive the series.'

'What about *Corrie*?'

'Yes, that Ena Sharples sure can dish it out.'

So, please, no hints about how *Brideshead* finishes, or whether Hugh Laurie cheers up. And not a word about how the Brits did at Wimbledon. I've got the whole thing stacked up on my PVR and will watch it in its entirety in 2015.

21–27 July

Driven to despair

Rental cars? Don't get me started . . .

For once, a piece of genuinely useful advice. I honestly expect to get letters in future from people saying, 'Thanks, Eddie – that really helped.' So stay tuned, as we say on the radio.

My story begins, as all good stories do, at the car-rental desk of an airport somewhere in the sunny Med. In my experience, car-rental staff seem sad all the time. Not just a bit down; I mean country-song sad. They've shuffled in to work despite their partner running off with their best friend, their dog dying and their TV being locked onto endless repeats of *Piers Morgan Tonight*. There's a deadness behind their eyes that puts me in mind of . . . well, Piers Morgan.

So imagine my delight when my rental-car person deadpanned that I'd been given an upgrade. I never rent anything grander than a class-B car, because I believe all the government advice about it inevitably leading to reliance on class-A cars. On the plus side, I benefit from spending almost nothing on a week's rental. The downside is, the vehicle is the size of a melon and has a sewing machine for an engine.

'An upgrade? Me?' I trilled, as the rental-car person wept uncontrollably into my paperwork. He scribbled the number of my parking bay on the damp document and handed me the keys bearing the logo of the manufacturer: BMW. The underground parking garage was gloomier than Jack Dee reading the July weather forecast. It was dark and stiflingly hot, but I found my Beemer, got in the wrong side, then got in the right side and prepared to turn on the air-con and drive off.

BMW drivers reading this will know what's coming. I couldn't start the car. The key-type item in my hand had no key on it, and my preliminary fumbling round the steering column betrayed no slot in which to shove it. There was a start button, but pressing that only put the lights on. Where was the slot for the dongly thing?

Minutes went by. My hands felt frantically around the driver's side for anything that might work. The heat and the lack of air-con, combined with a rising sense of panic, brought me out in a sweat. And I felt daft for not being able to perform a simple task. I haven't felt so stupid since saying to Caroline Thomson, 'Don't worry, love, you're a shoo-in for D-G'. I sat there repeating this pointless searching over and over.

Presently, a woman in the people carrier next door tapped on the window. 'Are you having trouble?' I explained my predicament and together we fumbled round the infrastructure in search of the necessary slot, but to no avail. Her husband suggested pressing the brake at the same time as the start button, but no. The instruction manual was in Spanish.

Eventually, a car-rental employee walked past. I waved frantically. She looked at me as if I was a red, sweat-soaked buffoon. 'You don't insert key. Just press clutch and start at same time.' Yes, BMW invented a car with a key you never need to insert, though I knew where I wanted to insert it.

I hope this helps you.

4–10 August

Flipping nightmare

Why I used the f-word and the c-word on TV

'I'm happy to approve the f***, but it requires your approval for the c***.'

The trial of John Terry for a racially aggravated public order offence was a tricky one for the news media. Awareness of the strong language used on the football field that day, and then in a public courtroom for a week, was critical to understanding the legal arguments. But how the heck do you properly convey those flipping words without causing offence?

I was bamboozled by some of the press coverage. One paper's copy looked like an explosion in an asterisk factory. Working out some of the sweary bits was worse than Sudoku. Another paper just went for it and printed every doggone word. I know it was a desperately serious case, but there was something vaguely thrilling about seeing Roger Mellie from *Viz* doing court reporting, and it was only through the unasterisked version that I really got a grasp of the details.

It's not possible to eff and blind your way through a radio news programme – think what the Secretary of State for Media would have to say about it. I know that at the BBC there was a lot of discussion about how to proceed. An early attempt had us broadcasting a warning about strong language, only to follow it with the words: 'effing black c-word'. Sometimes the words weren't indicated at all. It was especially tricky on radio, where there is no defined watershed.

My experience of Radio 4 listeners is that they like to be treated like grown-ups. We once got complaints about a piece of audio that was judged to have been bleeped so excessively all meaning was lost. 'Let us hear the swearing,' we were told. And generally, if a clear warning is given, and the use of the strong language is deemed necessary, people are happy to hear it.

The night Mr Terry was cleared, I happened to be presenting *Newsnight*, on account of the under-reported but serious national presenter shortage. We spent much of the day wrestling with how to convey the legal judgment. We were on well after the watershed and on BBC2, but there was no certainty about what to do. There was a flurry of emails between executives, including the one I quoted at the top of this column. It was all the more stark in its unasterisked form. It still makes me laugh to read it, but behind it lies the deadly serious desire to inform properly without gratuitously offending.

We decided to do a slightly provocative opening to *Newsnight* with me, on screen, using the infamous phrase. We would not only bleep the strong language, but also blur my lips to bamboozle even the most gifted lip-reader. This was how the football footage of John Terry had been treated all week and we thought it appropriate.

When we came to record the opening to be 'bleeped and blobbed', we were so sensitive about using the original phrase in front of a mic that the words I actually uttered were 'flipping black cult'. And even after the bleeping, we had a discussion about whether it was appropriate to hear the final 't'.

I think we probably got the balance right, to use that over-used phrase. If we hadn't, we'd have been deep in the shot.

18–24 August

I'm just the new boy

But it's time to let out some Newsnight *secrets*

The *Newsnight* green room is a mysterious place. It's a windowless tomb, in the basement of BBC Television Centre, about so big by so big. There are a couple of sofas, some chairs, a fridge and some stand-alone shelves with trinkets on, which may have been rescued from a 1983 *Blue Peter* set makeover. It's a place where the production team can take studio guests after the programme to thank them for schlepping out at this hour to appear on TV.

The room is impossible to find unaided. It's miles from both the production office and the studio and is tucked away discreetly up a narrow corridor off a winding corridor that looks the same as every other corridor. It has been a complete surprise to me every time a colleague has said, 'Here we are'. And there's a four-digit pin code for the door, which I haven't been given, and 'never will'.

It was in this room, just before the start of the 2012 Olympics, that a guest revealed his plan to avoid the Games altogether. For the duration, he was booked to stay in Las Vegas. He wanted to be miles from the throng, enormous travel delays and grinding security problems. He would spend a fortnight or so in a windowless tomb, about so big by so big, asking a croupier to hit him.

I wonder now whether he regrets his decision. He missed something special. What happened to us all during these Olympics? In our production offices at work, where the TVs are normally tuned to twenty-four-hour news and the people talk animatedly about whether quantitative easing will be expanded, everyone became an ill-informed sports expert.

'I think it was a world record but not an Olympic record.' 'Didn't they just cross the line? Why are they still cycling? Oh, another lap?' 'Wait . . . why did they change strokes half-way through the medley?'

At random moments, there would be cheering, gasping or even roaring in our normally erudite surroundings. I even heard Martha Kearney blurt out 'Keep going!' at her TV monitor during a particularly exciting race. Luckily, listeners to *The World at One* merely thought she was asking a guest to continue.

Now it's over and the world seems a duller place. I did a straw poll of the *Newsnight* studio audience and almost all of them said they enjoyed the Games. Yes, that's right, there's a live studio audience for *Newsnight*. It's one of TV's biggest secrets.

You can only get a ticket if you know who to ask. I do not know who to ask, and 'never will', but somehow each night three hundred news fans queue up dutifully to watch the programme go out. They're instructed not to applaud, cough or laugh at any point, lest they let the cat out of the bag. I'll probably get into trouble for revealing this, but I thought you should know.

I can't wait to see the official BBC response. It will either be a strict 'no comment' or 'Eddie was just trying to make a joke'. They're all in on it. The ticket money is used to stock the green-room fridge.

25–31 August

A shocking truth

Kirsty Wark's cattle-prod secret is safe with me

It's holiday time for many people, and TV and radio presenters are just like many people, except they tend to wear make-up all the time. Especially the radio presenters. The faces and voices you're accustomed to are sunning their make-up on tropical beaches and so, just as when flu sweeps London's theatreland, it's suddenly stand-ins everywhere.

I've been having fun of late deputising on *Newsnight* on BBC2 and *Any Questions?* on Radio 4. The upside of doing *Newsnight* is that its offices are directly across the corridor from the office where Radio 4's daily news and current affairs programmes, like *PM*, are made. As long as I remember to turn left and not right on my way in to TV Centre, everything is fine. And it all was fine apart from the night I took a wrong turning and accidentally presented five minutes of *The World Tonight*. Robin Lustig was unflappable, of course, and didn't baulk at me introducing the report on the rise of the right in Uzmenistan and the pressure on all sides in the capital, Uzmenibad.

The only downside of doing *Newsnight* is that it's on so late. During the Olympics it was on even later. The production team are all night owls, but I'm more of a morning person. This led to judicious use of a cattle prod on at least two occasions on the set to keep me awake. Why Kirsty Wark keeps a cattle prod in the office was never explained to me, but it did the trick and the viewers didn't notice, aside from a faint plume of black smoke emanating from my rump. There was a slightly startled look about my eyes but, frankly, I have that all the time after 9 p.m.

Newsnight is just across the corridor, but *Any Questions?* demands travel. Long before the BBC decided to move thousands of its staff outside London, the *AQ* team have been taking it to the people – travelling to every cranny and nook in the kingdom. I'll swear there isn't a school or village hall that has not played host to the programme, or my name isn't Cindy-Lou Peebles. There's something charming about preparing for a programme in a classroom festooned with the colourful drawings created by five-year-olds, or in a tiny room off a main church hall that is busy with parish announcements and details of fund-raising successes.

The financial cost of taking a programme like *Any Questions?* on the road each week is quite high. I can imagine an accountant working out that it would save squillions by broadcasting from one set venue each week. And the lazy part of me would like nothing better than to cross the corridor to do the programme. But the value of meeting your audience, and people, no matter where they live, having the chance to take part in the programme, is incalculable. When I interviewed Nicholas Parsons for *Radio Times* recently, he was bemoaning the fact that cuts meant *Just a Minute* was on the road less frequently. That is a shame. Giving people the chance to be part of our programmes on their own doorsteps is a great way of having them connect with their BBC.

1–7 September

Emergency Service

Eddie Mair tracks down the RT *readers whose lives were changed forever by Lord Reith's SOS messages*

This week I spent some time standing in front of the portrait of Lord Reith, the BBC's first director-general, at Broadcasting House. I noticed a number of things. Sartorial standards in the Corporation have slipped somewhat since Lord Reith's day. He never remembered to wear his BBC pass. I have a lot less paperwork to worry about than he did, and I will soon have the same amount of hair.

What, you may ask, was I doing goofing around in the hallowed Council Chamber, under the portrait of the man credited with fashioning the public-service broadcasting ethos that still pulses through today's BBC?

The story began in the pages of *Radio Times*. A while back I wondered whether readers had any recollections of the SOS messages that I remember from years gone by. They always seemed to be on just before the news. In sparse language and serious tones they shone a brief, bright light on some unfolding human drama. 'Would Mr and Mrs John Smith, believed to be travelling around Cumbria in an Austin Maxi, please contact the hospital in Winchester where Mrs Ethel Smith is dangerously ill.' A telephone number would be read out, and that was it.

We were all left to wonder, while the pips played and the news began, whether Mr and Mrs Smith ever made it to that far-off bedside. Would poor Ethel die alone? Perhaps she pulled through and would go on to die in a freak accident forty years later, run over by a car driver distracted by an SOS message on the radio.

We were never told. SOS messages were the most intense, personal moments in broadcasting. They used the power of radio and its ability to reach millions instantly to reach out to one or two individuals to tell them something that mattered only to them. But what happened to those people, we never knew. Which is why I asked *RT* readers for their experiences.

There was a big reaction. Many readers recalled hearing the messages. Others found themselves in the position of rushing to bedsides. One reader was a young girl when she fell very ill and an appeal was made for her parents to return home.

It was 1958 and six-year-old Linda Miller was staying with her auntie while her parents went off on holiday to London. Linda became very ill with what was initially suspected to be polio, but turned out to be a bone infection. She was taken into hospital in Sunderland, while an SOS message was broadcast in the hope of finding her parents.

They never heard it. But thankfully a cyclist by the name of Mr Clampit did. He remembered the details of their number plate from the broadcast and tapped on the car window when he spotted the vehicle in a car park. As a result, Mum and Dad made it to young Linda's bedside and, after several months of treatment, she was released from hospital and grew up to be the kind of beautiful person who buys *Radio Times*.

I was moved by much of what I heard and I wish we'd had more time on air to dwell on their experiences. People were happy to share some personal, life-changing moments, and I want to thank here everyone who wrote, and everyone to whom we spoke.

The BBC archive revealed a great deal I didn't know. For instance, the SOS system dated back to the earliest days of the British Broadcasting Company in the twenties. John Reith saw the public-service possibilities of the messages and helped craft the rules that governed them. While the initial broadcasts could include missing persons (and pets), the system was honed to target only those who were dangerously ill. I know some people suspect 'dangerously ill' was code for a person who had already died, but that's an urban myth. There were strict rules to ensure that, just before an SOS message was broadcast, a phone call was made to the hospital in question to ensure that the subject of the message was still with us. If the person had died, the message was cancelled.

Messages could be broadcast only once. No exceptions. And the BBC judged that it would be wrong to broadcast any follow-up to an SOS message, which is why we remained in the dark about what happened next. Auntie Beeb was keen to protect the individuals involved from prying enquiries. But the archive reveals that checks were made internally on how many SOS messages were successful.

You may be pondering when you last heard an SOS message. Not in the past decade, certainly, but exactly when I don't know. Having successfully traced the birth of SOS messages thanks to the detailed paper trail that dates back to the BBC's first moments, there is no certainty about when or why they stopped. No sign of a memo axing them. We've asked the people who would know, but it seems a combination of emerging technology (mobile phones) and Radio 4 schedule changes meant there was no more need for those chilling broadcasts.

I learnt a few other things in making our programme. In a note from the archive, from 1923 or 1924, there was word of the *Daily Express* demanding that the BBC be closed down. *Plus ça change.* And I discovered that John Reith himself wrote a weekly column for *Radio Times*. Finally something I had in common with him, besides being Scottish. We wrote for the same magazine. And for the same fee.

20–26 October

Mair v Pesto: round 2

The feud erupts in 'Nam (that's Cheltenham)

Once again it was me versus Robert Peston. The venue? The Cheltenham Literary Festival. Face-off: Sunday, 2 p.m. Robert was due to appear in a small tent at that moment, discussing his latest tome, *How the Hell Did the Economy Get So Bad and Can I Fill a Book with It?* Meanwhile, in an ornate hall with a thousand seats, I was booked to host a *Radio Times*-sponsored event: Seven Hundred Years of *Desert Island Discs*, or something.

I'm thrilled to report our event was a sell-out, while Robert's, I am reliably informed, was sparsely attended, with only George Osborne, Ed Balls and a goat in the audience. I hope this doesn't come across as bitter. As you know, Robert and I had a long-running feud that we patched up when Robert very graciously agreed it was all his fault. We even presented an edition of *PM* together. But I'm afraid to report that Robert's new book, *No, Seriously, How Did This Happen?*, has opened up a new chasm of mistrust between us, into which he has poured all my hopes and dreams. And then set fire to them.

What's the problem?

Check the acknowledgements in *What on Earth Is Going On with the Economy? Really. I'm Not Kidding*, and you'll find a list of people being profusely thanked by the BBC's business editor. Huw Edwards is on the list. Tess Daly. Tyne Daly, Tom DeLay and Tom Daley. A host of BBC insiders get the thank-you treatment. But yours truly – the *only* person to have bothered to have a public feud with Robert – is missing.

I have resolved to remove all references to Robert from my own forthcoming volume, *My Feud with Robert Peston*, although my publisher has her doubts about the wisdom of that.

My Cheltenham session was a delight. Not because of me or anything I did, but because the audience loved *Desert Island Discs* and were there to show their appreciation for Kirsty Young, the programme's producer Leanne Buckle and Sean Magee who wrote the book *Desert Island Discs: Seven Thousand Years of Castaways*.

Kirsty revealed some secrets of the show (she's never done it sober), while Leanne let us in on her off-air troubles (Kirsty has never done the show sober). Sean was the real revelation, though. I thought I knew the story of the genesis of *Desert Island Discs*: Roy Plomley having the idea one night in the early forties. But I was wrong.

Although the first broadcast was in 1942, Mr Plomley had been performing *Desert Island Discs* in his front parlour since 1921. Family, friends and neighbours would be invited in once a week to choose their favourite discs. One sunny August afternoon in 1921, a young John Reith was passing the open window of Roy Plomley's house when he heard the fishmonger describe to Roy his desired Desert Island luxury.* The future BBC director-general knocked on the Plomley door and offered him a job there and then. Well, not quite there and then. The BBC hadn't started at that point and Reith hadn't been appointed. But Reith did promise him a series to start several years hence, 'perhaps during the war?' The rest is history.

---

* A fish slice.

27 October–2 November

My face opens doors

So why am I being turned away at the BBC gates?

A humiliating moment last week as I tried to enter New Broadcasting House in London. The security guard looked at my pass. And then looked some more. And then some more. 'It *is* me!' I offered, nervously.

'Yes. Perhaps a much *younger* version of you.'

Naturally, I was affronted. Then I looked at the photo on the pass. In fact I'm staring at it now. I look like a young East German shot-putter from 1976. One of the women.

The person in the photo doesn't have grey hair, nor dead eyes or wrinkles. I'm only sure it's me because I've been carrying the damn thing around for years. If you put the pass photo alongside a current snapshot, it resembles something you'd see in a newspaper ad for something horrendous. 'Has your life been horrifically damaged by breathing too much varnish? Look what it did to this man! Call us now and we'll get you a million pounds in compensation.'

It was nice of the security guard not to laugh in my face. How do people at passport control stop themselves from sniggering? The backs of their hands must be red-raw from pinching. They should be congratulated on their wills of steel – somehow not exploding in laughter as ageing, balding, bloated wrecks try to enter the country on passports bearing the likeness of lithe, hirsute, young bubblies.

I popped to the BBC ID unit to enquire about getting a new photo. That could be done right away, I was told, but it would take four days for my new pass to arrive, during which time I'd have no pass at all. I'd be unable to get into any BBC building, and even if I accomplished entry, it would be impossible to get in and out of secure areas. Such as studios.

Alive to this obvious drawback, the helpful young man in the ID unit (who probably does still look like his pass photo) explained that people tend to order replacement passes just before they go on holiday. They come back from their break looking significantly older – like plastic surgery in reverse. I might remember that handy tip. Or I might carry on walking round with a photo of Olga Fraukop Schlurpidonger around my neck.

Exodus from TV Centre

I hardly ever wear make-up on radio, but TV demands it. As the make-up artists trowel on the factor 50, there's often a waspish remark or well-sourced bit of tittle-tattle. It's great fun. But times are changing. The last time I hosted *Newsnight* (and they were quite clear it would be the *last* time) was the penultimate edition from TV Centre. Now, Jeremy and Co. come atcha from central London. TV Centre is increasingly empty these days and my make-up woman was wistful. She'd trained in the building and was sad to see its echoing, empty corridors and offices.

I didn't have the heart to say I'd just been at New Broadcasting House, whose make-up rooms seem four floors below ground, devoid of natural light and with barely a person in sight. On the plus side a dizzying spiral staircase is the only way to reach the corridor and your light-headedness by the time you reach −4 is quite satisfying. Like smelling too much varnish.

17–23 November

Bash to the boss

Sometimes you have to settle a few scores . . .

It was a regular Thursday afternoon in the *PM* office. As usual our 5 p.m. deadline was hurtling towards us like a sharp blade in a knife-throwing act. Then the editor of *The World at One* turned round from his desk to say 'Are any of you listening to Danny Baker? It's amazing.'

It's not uncommon for him to pipe up with unusual questions, so we've learnt to take them with a pinch of salt. Have we seen what Sharon Gless is wearing in *Hello!*? What happened in *Zorro* last night? What are wasps for?

It usually falls to poor Martha Kearney to come up with the answers, but on this particular day she'd gone home to deal with a bee-related emergency. As you know, Martha keeps bees and is rarely seen without a mini-swarm around her noggin. Listeners have written in to complain about high levels of interference on long wave during *The World at One* but it's just her bees making a racket. They adore her, as do we all, but someone needs to tell her that it's beginning to affect the programme. And devoting *The World at One*'s extra fifteen minutes a day to honey-related recipes? Is no one going to stop that?

We turned our dials to BBC London 94.9 and found that on this occasion the tip from the *WATO* editor was spot on. Danny Baker was live on air in full flow, railing against a decision by management to get rid of his daily 3–5 p.m. show. It seems he'd found out about this shortly before going on air and was using the opportunity to speak candidly to his audience about what he believed were the shortcomings of the people running BBC London. It was fantastic radio. I don't normally catch Danny's show on account of being secured to a giant circular piece of plywood and spun repeatedly in a circle at that time of day. But this performance was unmissable and I've been trying to assess why.

It wasn't just because it was Danny Baker. He's articulate, funny and insightful on anything he does. Certainly there was something about him having all his broadcasting gifts zero in relentlessly on one target for two hours, and the passion and humour he used as weapons. There were the gripping glimpses behind the scenes at the station where he said 'everyone plainly hates each other'. And as the BBC wrestles with revelations about some of the darkest areas of human behaviour, these revelations were, by comparison, charmingly old-fashioned. This was classic radio in the style of DLT's on-air resignation from Radio 1 almost twenty years previously.

But perhaps we were just relishing someone doing what we've all considered at some point, regardless of our station in life. Who among us hasn't thought about winning the lottery and then going in to work to settle a few scores with our bosses? I couldn't be happier with my bosses in BBC News, namely Steve Mitchell and Helen Boaden, but sometimes you're forced to work with people who are precisely the pinheaded weasels Mr Baker described. Was Danny speaking for all of us? Doing something we can't – or won't. Letting out that rage in the style of the mad prophet of the airwaves, Howard Beale?

I'm mad as hell, too, but I'm out of space.

24–30 November

Whoops apocalypse

The BBC apologises for its latest blunder . . .

As I write this, the BBC is still broadcasting. Hold on, let me turn on the radio just to double-check. Yes, it's still broadcasting. Possibly by the time you read this it will not be. Perhaps you should turn on your radio just to double-check. I'll give you time.

Are we still on? Or was there white noise or birdsong? Or Peter Donaldson's voice on a loop announcing that Britain is about to be attacked by nuclear weapons? I understand that many years ago Peter had to make a recording to be played in the event of an impending catastrophe. Perhaps, in keeping with recent BBC style, it was broadcast accidentally, thus triggering a nuclear war that has ravaged the planet. In which case, thank you for your continued loyalty to *RT*. Other listings magazines are no longer available.

Tell me, what is happening in your post-apocalyptic world? I assume *The Archers* is still going on long wave. Did the massive loss of human life put a dent in the rehearsals for this year's Lynda Snell Christmas spectacular? Can Tom Archer's sausages still claim to be organic, despite the off-the-scale levels of radiation poisoning?

It would, of course, be entirely fitting for an erroneous BBC broadcast to spell the end of life as we know it. In those circumstances, there really would be a case for a public inquiry. The Corporation's critics would have a field day but, as ever, the BBC would be toughest on itself. John Humphrys, who survived the attack unscathed despite being at its hypocentre, would berate the director-general for the fatal broadcast.

> *Humphrys: Why was the wrong thing broadcast? Surely someone at the BBC can tell the difference between a recording labelled 'Jenni Murray's 50 Things to Do with Spam', and 'Peter Donaldson's End of the World Tape Only to Be Played in the Event of the End of the World'?*

D-G: Well, John, it's a good question. First, let me say that I am as appalled as you about this very serious error. I don't seek to make excuses for something that has wiped out most of the human race, destroyed most animal life and seriously undermined the case for the licence fee, but I think it should be acknowledged that this would probably not have happened had almost all the BBC's staff not been on gardening leave to allow them to prepare for the 246 separate inquiries into our other blunders. Naturally, I deeply regret every death, and rest assured I have asked Ken MacQuarrie from BBC What Remains of Scotland to have a report on the pile of ash that was my desk by Monday morning.

> *Humphrys: But won't many people be incredulous at what sounds like a classically complacent BBC response to a crisis that is of your making?*

D-G: We are going to do everything in our power to put this right. Tomorrow's *Farming Today* will include tips on how to sell charred wool. The surviving cast member of *EastEnders* (Adam Woodyatt) will incorporate public health messages into his monologue, and that Jenni Murray show will finally be aired – and I think we'll all find that very useful.

15–21 December

Manhattan transfer

My mission to be the new Alistair Cooke

Greetings from New York. Yes, I am communicating with you directly from the city in which Alistair Cooke composed his *Mainly About Manhattan* broadcasts in the late thirties: the forerunner to his longer-lasting *Letters*. And, in tribute, this week's column will be mainly about Manhattan. What a treat for us both, and you can be sure I have the wit, warmth and intelligence to match Mr Cooke in a column that will sparkle with his trademark wisdom and erudition.

Everyone loves a critic

I went to see an off-Broadway musical yesterday whose main song had the word **** in the title.

I realise you're now trying to identify the word, and my lack of clues is an annoying hindrance to that end. But I cannot hint at it further, given that it's widely deemed to be perhaps the most offensive word in the English language. Revealing the rest of the song title would in all likelihood cause as much offence as the word itself. If you really want to know more, search online for *Silence! The Musical* – but only if you are prepared to be very, very offended.

It is indeed an unofficial parody of *Silence of the Lambs*. Two minutes in, you're wondering why the creators weren't sued by the *Lambs* people, and after thirty minutes the aforementioned grossly offensive song has become your filthiest-ever earworm. But it was a bloody funny show.

Killing time in my taxi from hell

Getting from a New York airport to Manhattan has in the past involved being squished in the back of a yellow cab with less legroom than the economy flight out. I tend to get the driver who's taking a holiday from hygiene and has a trigger-happy horn finger. I was determined that this trip I would arrive in comfort. I got the hotel to pre-book what was described as a 'town car'. It would cost more than the flight, but I was determined for once to have a smooth ride.

Stepping into the vehicle I wondered which town the town car hailed from. Wigan? The driver clearly had a passion for tobacco and, I judged, taking Labradors on long journeys to and from the beach. He had a nice line in New York patter (jokes/comedy accents of all kinds/incontrovertible wisdom on politics) that began when we first met and continued uninterrupted until I threw his dead body into the Hudson.

A room with a view

After checking in, the receptionist was unsurprised to get a call from me asking why the air-conditioning unit was hanging off the wall allowing the howling wind into the room. Classily, she moved me to a room next to the lifts.

Shop 'til you drop

There are three men on the TV right now, in footage of a fist-fight in the post-Thanksgiving sales. They appear to be trying to kill each other over some bargain women's underwear. I can vouch for the viciousness of some Manhattan shoppers. I've never seen such pushing, shoving and animal-like aggression. It made me sad for the human race to witness such a lack of humanity. On the other hand, I did beat all those suckers to the best of the sales and saved eight bucks.

2013

Gone missing

The truth behind Radio 4's lost voices

So many familiar and beloved voices have disappeared from Radio 4 in recent days that people keep coming up to me and asking, 'Why are you still on the network?'

And it's true I have only a few months to serve until that inevitable call to the office of whoever is in charge by that stage, who will mumble something about 'Nothing to do with you ... marvellous contribution ... refresh the schedule ... talentless prat' and I, too, will be off.

But for now we mourn the (Radio 4) passing of Sir Peter Donaldson (as he will surely be known), Dame Charlotte Green, Dame Harriet Cass and Dame Alice Arnold. Peter has done his last shift. Charlotte's final newsreading stints on *PM* were last week. Between them those four voices have served the nation with more than two thousand years of broadcasting. They've announced shipping forecasts, wars, famines, royal babies, gale warnings (when did you last hear one of those?) and all the greyhound results. No, wait, that's just what Harriet does in the office every afternoon. She's a fiend for her doggy racing and I'm told has her own box at Yarmouth.

After people have asked me what I'm still doing on the network, the next thing they ask is why all these voices – the very essence of the network – are disappearing pretty much at the same time. I used to say they were all being replaced by Clare Balding, but that's no longer funny.

Regular readers will remember I revealed the truth behind this Beeb Bloodbath some time ago. In essence, they're all being fired for stealing things from work. Peter's house was raided and they found boxes and boxes of staples. But not a single stapler. Apparently it was a cry for help. At Alice's house they found reams of blank headed notepaper from every director-general since the early 1930s. It seems she would use them to get free flight upgrades, thanks in part to her uncanny resemblance to Lord Reith. They struggled to push open Harriet's front door, but when they did they found thousands of unbroadcast gale warnings. And when they showed up at Charlotte's it turned out she'd managed to steal the whole of Radio 3. Happily this has all been hushed up by the BBC's now-defunct 'keeping things out of the papers' department, and all four have got lucrative other work lined up.

Peter couldn't resist an offer to become the new face and voice of Captain Birdseye. He already has the look, and promises to bring his distinguished tones to the part. I understand that in future the Captain's Table will be festooned not only with crunchy 100 per cent cod fish fingers but also fine Merlot.

Harriet, Charlotte and Alice will be appearing in an updated version of *The Golden Girls* for Gold. There is some squabbling over casting as no one wants to be Sophia but it's got hit, or something like that, written all over it.

It's very sad to see them all go. I'll miss them at work and miss hearing them on the radio. They are Radio 4. And they're every bit as fun to be around as you would imagine. Except Charlotte. There was some talk of them all being replaced by Heather Bell, who's returning to *The Archers* to take over her old role as Clarrie Grundy, but it came to nothing.

16–22 February

Through the roof

The soothing ups . . . and deadly downs of lift travel

A friend of mine once got stuck in a lift with Piers Morgan. When the man on the other end of the emergency telephone told her that a rescue would take an hour and a half, she immediately crunched down on the cyanide capsule she carried, as many others do, in case they're stuck in a lift with Piers Morgan. What a senseless waste of human life.

I'm kidding of course. There was no cyanide capsule. But my friend did die. On the death certificate where the doctor indicates the cause of death, there was a single word: 'boredom' – though the coroner also noted the frantic scratch marks all over the interior of the lift.

Thankfully there is no such risk in the exciting new world of lifts that awaits you at New Broadcasting House in central London. There are four situated either side of the swanky new entrance, making a total of eight: nine if you count the lift that's for the sole use of the director-general. Its precise location is such a closely guarded secret that it's known only to the seventy-three people who've done the job in 2012/13. Rumour has it the lift is made of glass and can go up, down, sideways and through the roofs, just like the D-G! The manufacturers didn't think anyone would be able to afford it, but there's always some Wonka at the BBC with more money than sense.

The wondrous thing about the eight lifts for the use of mere mortals is that each one has piped into it the output of a BBC radio station. There is a sign on the wall of each lift alerting you to which network it is. You can arrive at work to the sounds of Radio 2. Pop out for lunch accompanied by BBC London and return to something wonderful on 5 Live. The thing is, it's pot luck which lift comes first and therefore which network you get.

As you know, I'm a people watcher (the court called it something else, but lawyers can twist anything) and I take particular pleasure in monitoring the reaction of BBC types as they crowd into a given network's lift. Young trendies in their uber-fashionable clothes wince when confronted with three floors of Radio 4. Similarly, grey-haired types with beards and tweed jackets have been seen putting their fingers in their ears as the doors close on the 1Xtra lift. I even saw one executive hovering endlessly at the lift concourse, explaining, 'I'm waiting for the Radio 3'. It's certainly the most restful lift. I only have to go three floors but all I've ever heard in it is meaningful silences.

The lifts are particularly crowded between five and six on a weekday evening. Some say this is because it's the time when many staffers are heading home. But I believe it's down to folk stepping in to go a few floors but being so mesmerised by the wonderful content in the Radio 4 lift that they choose to ride up and down for an hour rather than miss a word.

Is there medication for these delusions of mine? Almost certainly. And I would happily take the pills, were it not for my fear of accidentally mixing them up with my Piers Morgan capsule.

Anyway, it'll all be academic when the new D-G arrives in April. Apparently he wants every lift to be blasted with something from the bloody opera.

2–8 March

Sunday service

I reap the perks of standing in for Andrew Marr

Every Sunday morning at nine on Radio 4 there's an excellent programme called *Paddy O'Connell's Broadcasting House with Me, Paddy O'Connell*. Younger listeners may not realise that, for the first few years of the show, Paddy had to have stand-ins on account of his being in a 'facility'. He's fine now and rarely misses a performance but it used to fall to me or Fig Lover to step in and do the honours.

While standing in for Paddy had its compensations (free newspaper ink on your hands and a fighting chance of sharing the croissant the BBC provides for the host and all the guests), there was no real pleasure in getting up before 6 a.m. and driving to work as drunk people walked in the opposite direction. I can tell you that by the time Paddy got the all-clear, it was a blessed relief to both Fig and me. We had our Sunday mornings back! So it was with mixed feelings that I took a call recently from the good people at *The Andrew Marr Show*.

To be serious for a moment, it was a shock to all when Andrew suffered a stroke, and Sundays aren't the same without him. We all wish him well and can't wait to have him back on the airwaves. A whole pile of BBC people have been doing a fine job deputising for him and I didn't really expect to be added to the list.

But, as the *Marr* people kindly revealed during the phone call, there was absolutely no one else available for the third weekend in February. Apparently it was me or dead air. The dilemma had gone all the way up to the acting director-general and I understand it was finally decided on a coin-toss. So I'm now in a position to reveal the behind-the-scenes secrets of Sunday morning's most-watched-programme-that's-not-pretending-to-be-even-a-little-bit-about-religion.

First of all, they have great offices. Some central parts of New Broadcasting House are as far from natural daylight as a cow in Debbie's mega-dairy on *The Archers*. It can resemble a call centre. I swear I passed the desks of *The World Tonight* and heard a producer on the phone offering substantial discounts if the person on the other end would take dual-fuel by direct debit.

The *Marr* team, by contrast, have a well-lit corner office with views up the tree-lined streets to Regent's Park. There are bookshelves. It is paradise. I can quite see why Andrew rushes to the office each week on that scooter of his.

Which brings me to another true story. The stand-in presenters have access to that scooter. Most take up the offer, except Sian Williams, who uses her own Harley-Davidson. I was nervous, after a serious fall I suffered some years ago from a bike. Actually, it might have been an elephant. Either way, it was outside a supermarket and a waste of 2p.

Citing my safety concerns, I asked for a scooter driver. Letting someone else drive was a masterstroke. I was able to spend time thumbing through the papers, then wolfed down the on-board yogurt muesli breakfast provided. I arrived at the office safely and on time, though my face was pebble-dashed with uncooked rolled oats and I stank of strawberries. No wonder guest Iain Duncan Smith looked at me funny.

9–15 March

I'm a frantic faffer

The biggest BBC scandal since the last one

If I had a penny for every time someone has asked for my thoughts about the publication of those Pollard Inquiry transcripts, I'd have a fortune – enough to pay for five minutes of the Pollard Inquiry. But I've batted away every polite question with my usual mix of either a beguiling smile, an enigmatic comment or a punch to the thorax. I was anxious to share my views exclusively with you. You should be the first to read my trenchant opinions about the biggest BBC scandal since the last one.

Strictly speaking, you're not the first to read these words. Before they reach your dazzling eyes, I always have to share my words with someone at the BBC who checks I'm not causing the organisation (further) embarrassment. Then there's the *Radio Times* editor, who ponders proofs of this page while lounging in his leather armchair, Pimm's in each hand, sucking on a fat Cuban. And finally there are the lawyers, who make sure I'm not libelling anyone who might sue.

But after them, you are the first and I intend to let loose. You deserve nothing better than the unvarnished truth. Those transcripts were intended to begin the healing process at the BBC – help bring people together and move on from a traumatic period. I couldn't agree more and am anxious to lift my eyes to the horizon, and away from the infighting portrayed in some of the pages.

It's worth considering though – who the ▧▧▧ does ▧▧▧ ▧▧▧ think he is? I read his testimony and thought: wow. I used to respect you and now I see you're a complete ███. And a ███ one at that. Unbelievable. Here's what I would like to see happen to ███ ███. I would take a sharp ███ and a blunt ███ and proceed to ███ his ███ until it wouldn't work even with immediate medical attention.

Golly gosh that feels better. Perhaps the whole unpleasantness caused you to reflect on how you would appear to the world if the content of your work email inbox were released for everyone to read. Mine would consist of appeals for cash, rants at the world and a stream of bad language. No, wait, that's my sent folder.

One final thought. A comment by the man who chairs the BBC Trust, Lord Patten, brought back happy memories. He said there was an impression of 'frantic faffing about' around George Entwistle. And suddenly I was back in the early days of *Broadcasting House* on Radio 4. It was the week before Christmas and nothing was happening in the world. We were desperate for something to put on the radio. In the Commons, some MP had said it was time for the government to stop faffing about. I jokingly suggested in the office that we should do a discussion on when it was appropriate to faff about and when it was time to stop.

Perhaps it was the looming deadline. Perhaps we were all hungover. But in the end we were phoning up potential guests, inviting them to appear on the radio debating the critical question gripping the nation: when should we stop faffing? It's a source of pride and shame in equal measure that together we made twenty minutes of entirely acceptable radio that started out as a joke. But I'm sure a historical re-examination of our emails would reveal a different story.

6–12 April

Boris: my regrets

Forget the interview – what about my bald spot?

I would like to start with an apology. This week's column was to have contained news of an exciting scientific break-through. For many months I have been working feverishly (but very privately) in the same area as the Large Hadron Collider people. They believe they may have glimpsed the Higgs boson particle. With all due respect to their talent, I have to tell you they are WAY behind me on this.

Not only have I glimpsed the particle, I have captured it and have it next to me here in a jar. It is my crowning achievement and I'd planned to make my historic announce-ment right here in a column dedicated to revealing just how I did it.

But yesterday I had a late-night caller who implored me to write about something else. It was the editor of *Radio Times*. Obviously he looks nothing like the heavily photoshopped mugshot he puts on page three. I recognised him only from the smell of Pimm's and regret. I'm not great with accents, but if you imagine a cross between Mike Reid and Arthur Mullard you'd be in the right area.

"'Ere, Eddie. You're packin' a lot of 'eat at the moment. 'Bout blaady time. Forget all that Henry Higgins stuff you're plannin'. Gimme the dirt on Boris!' He planted a fat Cuban in my hand and limped off into the night chuckling maniacally.

And so, having started with an apology, I'd like to intro-duce another. You already kindly put up with my mugshot at the top of my column and perhaps occasionally catch me droning on the radio. So I'm sorry that in recent days my fizzog has been popping up in newspapers, magazines and on tea towels. I'm only pleased that what doctors feared was a frightening surge in cases of *Clostridium difficile* could in fact be traced to the public's reaction to my sudden ubiquitousness.

One of the joys of live broadcasting is that you never have to hear or see your work unless you really go out of your way. You prepare it, do it, then head to the bar. Well, that's usually the order. But last week there was, for a moment, no avoiding screengrabs and clips of the eminent and likeable Boris Johnson being badgered by a balding sack of potatoes in a cheap suit. Yes, balding. And not the nice Clare kind.

Never mind all the stuff about what the interview revealed. The photos revealed something very shocking to me. What in my mind was my discreet but manageable bald spot is in fact the size of a dinner plate. Only the over-the-shoulder TV camera angle could tell me this and, what's worse, it was then relayed in every newspaper in the land.

I could play a monk in a low-budget TV movie. You could sell advertising space on it (note to self: check with BBC lawyers whether this might be do-able for my next Marr stand-in).

As for all the hullaballoo ... for the record, I don't want Jeremy's job. Or John's. Or Andrew's. I like mine. Though my contract is up soon and I haven't heard anything, so if you run a radio or TV station and you think there's a future for a forty-seven-year-old in a bad wig – call my agent.

13–19 April

For auld lang syne

Leaving parties spell white wine and regret . . .

My day yesterday had a whiff of nostalgia about it. I thought at first it was a whiff of wet clothing, on account of being caught in the rain again during this Narnia winter we're all enjoying so much, but no, it was nostalgia. It still lingers. I've a feeling I might drift into sepia-toned mellowness that may cause nausea.

It started around 3 p.m. I was at my desk, weeping openly as per, when an entirely unexpected figure hove into view across the familiar sea of computer terminals, piles of newspapers and weeping producers. That thick mane of greying hair – so large it has its own postcode, so treasured it is a UNESCO World Heritage Site – could only belong to one man: Peter Allen, from Radio 5 Live's *Drive*. Peter, along with many others from that network, has been working out of Salford for years, after a little-known poker bet by Mark Thompson went badly awry.

In the early nineties, when 5 Live launched, Peter and I worked in the same room at Broadcasting House in London. My most treasured memories are of covering party conferences with him year after year. He would do the early shift and me the late. He is as switched-on and smart as the best of them, but also a hilarious delight to work with. All I can remember is Peter constantly making me laugh. He was and is the best at this game, and although his show is on at the same time as *PM* I have no hesitation in recommending it to you warmly. (I'm a bit nauseous myself now. When will this niceness stop?)

There Peter was at my desk. We hugged, insulted each other, cried a little (I may have wet myself a bit) and I asked him what he was doing in London. He explained he was co-presenting his show from here, and later that evening would attend a leaving do for a retiring BBC executive.

'I'm going to the same do!' I said, and I could see the panic in Peter's eyes as he realised he might have to see me again later. He explained he was very busy/people to see/things to do and off he bustled until only his hair was visible, as it still is from space.

Later, the leaving bash itself was a treat. It was held in the BBC's inner sanctum – the Council Chamber of Broadcasting House. All the greats were there. John Humphrys. Jeremy Vine. Harriet Cass. Peter Donaldson. Brian Perkins. I'm just listing names now, but really, there were a lot of people you'd know. Nice speeches, a funny video, and genuine warmth and affection for the person who was leaving.

It's quite possible that you've never heard of him and he wouldn't mind if you hadn't. To look at his photograph – a grey-looking man – you'd perhaps assume he was the sort of BBC timeserver so easily mocked by the Corporation's critics. Given his thirty-eight years of service, he appears to fit the bill.

But the retiring deputy director of BBC News, Steve Mitchell, is the doughtiest exponent of the BBC's values I've known. Integrity. Decency. Honesty. I realise I'm just listing virtues now, but really, he is a person you should know the BBC will miss a great deal.

4–10 May

The view from here

My journey to the very top of the BBC

After almost five months in New Broadcasting House I went on an amazing adventure last week. I went to the seventh floor!

I realise this hardly qualifies me as broadcasting's Sir Ranulph Twisleton-Wykeham-Fiennes but you have to understand that New BH was designed to be a workplace for the twenty-first century, or something. Gone are those pesky twentieth-century irritants like offices and walls. Welcome to the brave new open-plan world where everything and everyone are visible at all times. Away with the silo mentality that meant you never physically saw people who worked on other programmes. Now you *can* see them! And look! They're looking back at you!

It's possible to stand by the glass overlooking the central atrium and watch someone on the second floor pick their nose. With proper timing, you can moon the weather presenter during the *News at Six* (though Martha has been told to stop doing this). On the third floor alone, in the space of a few seconds it's possible to walk from *PM* through *Andrew Marr, Newsnight, Newshour, The World Tonight* and *The World at One* and then back to *PM*. I do it all the time. It's brilliant. People think you're busy.

Last week as I wandered past the *Newsnight* people, wondering who had microwaved a balti, it occurred to me that in five months I had never been above the fourth floor. I'd been to −3, where the *Newsnight/Marr* studio is, and to −1, where the canteen is. The ground floor is where you come in and the third floor is where I 'work'. I'm only ever invited to the fourth floor when someone from management wants to make me feel like a worthless piece of trash.

But what strange worlds lay in the layers above floor four? With a sense of adventure not felt since the day I got into the lift with John Sweeney, I decided to grab the future with both hands, throw caution to the wind and head, arbitrarily, for the seventh floor. I'm not even sure how many floors there are but seven seemed a sensible compromise between my previous best (four) and going out through the roof in the glass elevator. Up and up I went, the air becoming thinner than my hair, until eventually, twelve or thirteen seconds later, the doors opened and there it was before my very eyes. The seventh floor.

It turns out it was just people sitting around staring at computers like on every other floor, so I went back down in the lift and thought no more about it.

Brief encounters

The open-plan arrangement means that senior people can suddenly appear at your shoulder without warning. Even Señor People from the Spanish Service can pop up when you least expect him.

This has happened to me twice in recent weeks. First, the new director-general Lord Hall appeared, with entourage. We shook hands, exchanged pleasantries, exchanged pastries and then he was whisked off to inspect the bum outline on the glass above the weather studio.

Last week I spied the incoming director of news, James Harding, heading our way (with smaller entourage) but his schedule didn't allow for a stop and chat this time. I heard his guide explaining, as they raced through, 'This is radio'.

18–24 May

My addled mind

Are musical incontinence pads the way forward?

These are strange times we're living in. Winter lasted until May. There are two popes. Everyone on TV is under arrest. It leads to a certain sense of discombobulation.

I couldn't feel more confused if I was a bagatelle ball. I feel like I'm in a constant helicopter downdraft. I feel like Telly Savalas's barber. I can't make any sense of the world any more. Increasingly I find myself starting off with one thought in my head and before I get to the end of the sentence I . . . musical incontinence pads that play 'Moon River' when they need changing.

Where was I? Yes. In order for the column to truly reflect my state of mind, it will consist entirely of sentences that have popped into my head in the last seven days. I don't make any great claims for them. Perhaps they're genius. Perhaps they're evidence I need to be sectioned under the Mental Health Act. Or both.

If I did a Freedom of Information request to the government to find out exactly what age 'women of a certain age' are, would I get an answer? I see cider adverts everywhere. There are big cider brands battling it out for market share. I don't drink cider but now I want to.

I am sitting in a restaurant, perusing the menu as I wait for my dining companion. Rather than ask the waiter what labneh is, I look it up on my smartphone. My phone is smarter than me.

My inner monologue needs new writers.

I read Julian Barnes's new book about love and grief and

am dazzled by his ability to reframe timeless universal experiences into new and thought-provoking sentences. It's a stunning piece of work.

Musical incontinence pads sound like a good idea, but in reality, who wants the world to know they've wet themselves?

I want William Shatner to live for ever.

Three years after getting specs for the first time – 'just for reading' – I can no longer leave the house without them. It makes me sad.

My whole life experience tells me that not fixing things in a timely fashion leads to greater trouble in future. The temperamental loo handle I ignored that finally gave up the ghost when I *really* needed to flush. The cracked car windscreen I dismissed as tiny that chose to shatter at 70 mph. Last night, just before bedtime, I noticed that the boiler is making a really loud noise, almost constantly. Yet I will do nothing about it.

I see a dog poop in the park. Its owner sees it too but doesn't bin the poop. I say nothing. It makes me sad. I read newspapers online during the week but at the weekend miss turning the pages.

I remember a wise teacher at school advising us not to make subject choices on the strength of being able to share a class with friends. I vividly recall him saying that we should choose subjects only because we wanted to. 'It might seem odd to you now, but thirty years from now you won't be able to remember five of your schoolfriends' names.' I try to remember the names of five school friends and can't. And I can't remember the name of the wise teacher either.

Is it worth maybe just approaching the estate of Andy Williams to sound them out?

8–14 June

Lost on *Newsnight*

I had to walk and talk without glasses

As I walk slowly towards death, the path is becoming more blurry. Regular readers will recall that a few years ago I had my first eye test since the Wilson administration. I was told I had a slight need for glasses to help me see long distances, and a desperate requirement for reading glasses. Strong ones. I seem to recall the Spanish-born optician ordering something for me from the 'microscopico' range.

This was my first foray into face furniture and it worked out better than I had anticipated. Before I got my specs I had three fears: (1) that I would break them; (2) lose them; (3) get confused between the distance and reading glasses and have a dreadful accident on the road or on air. To my surprise, I behaved like a grown-up and did not have a catastrophe.

But it was on the set of *Newsnight* one evening that I first realised one set of varifocals might be a better alternative. The thing about *Newsnight* is that you are sometimes required as a presenter to walk *and* talk at the same time. Late at night. On television. There's always a lot of faffing around sitting in one bit of the set, then striding awkwardly to a different set of seats. (It's all down to the BBC bean-counters, by the way. If you're not seen using all the studio floorspace provided, they can legally take it away. Ask Phillip Schofield about his broom-cupboard story.)

I didn't need glasses for the autocue, but I did need my readers to look at my interview notes. On air one evening, having sashayed successfully from one end of the set to the other, I realised to my horror that my all-important reading glasses were at the other desk. We were about to go live with a big discussion, but I was unable to read anything. I looked down at my notes and they were blurrier than the edges of Roobarb. Only a quick-thinking floor manager – every home should have one – saved me from resorting to my absolute fall-back in an on-air emergency: pretending to faint, Fawlty-style. Now I have several pairs of varifocals. When my eyes were tested again, the optician said my long-distance sight was deteriorating and she ordered something for me from the 'Hubble' range. I'm very happy. One pair does the job – although, as you'll know yourself if you're a varifocal person, you should never look at your feet when going downstairs. The distorting effect of the lens magnifies everything and your brain thinks you're drunk, often resulting in hilarious pratfalls. Certainly never wear varifocals, get drunk and look at your feet going downstairs. (Ask Phillip Schofield about his stairs to the broom-cupboard story.)

All of these horrors came to mind yesterday when an insurance company asked me to read the unique identification number (the IMEI, as it's known) from the back of my iPhone. Have you ever tried that? It's tiny black writing on a black background. I defy anyone to read it. If you don't have such a phone, go into a store and ask to read the IMEI number. You won't be able to. I squinted through every part of my specs. Screwed up my eyes. But nothing. It was impossible to read. I cancelled my plans to insure the device and called the optician instead.

29 June–5 July

Circus of life

It doesn't pay to dilly-dally in Piccadilly

It's Saturday afternoon and I'm waiting outside a theatre for my friend at Piccadilly Circus in London's glittering West End. The play, by the way, was huge fun: *The 39 Steps* at the Criterion. Four deft actors and about a million costume changes. People haven't removed their clothing so often in the West End since ... well, you can pretty much insert your own Raymond Revuebar joke here.

As I loiter, leaning against a wall opposite Eros, an odd feeling sweeps over me. It's the same feeling I get when I dream I'm five seconds away from going live on the radio and I look down to discover all my scripts are in Swahili. It's the same feeling I get when I see Martha Kearney walking towards me, her face almost obscured by a swarm of bees. It's the same feeling I get when I hear the words 'This is CNN. And now, for the whole of the next hour: Piers Morgan.'

I realise I'm standing still in an area most Londoners avoid or step through briskly. I've also just realised I appear to consider myself a Londoner. That's taken me by surprise. It brings to mind a not entirely serious chat with Scotland's First Minister as we prepared to record a down-the-line radio interview. It went like this:

Alex Salmond: 'Eddie, when are you coming back to live and work in Scotland?'

Me: 'When you get independence.'

Alex Salmond: 'Funny, that's just what Sean says.'

Where was I? Yes, I'm standing in a part of London alien

to locals. Foreign languages are everywhere as smiley visitors jostle for photographic position on the steps below the famous statue. There are also two cows milling around. (Can cows mill?)

In fact they're people dressed as cows and want to be hugged as part of a good-natured protest against slaughter-houses and in favour of veganism. I decline to hug either cow, in part because I must be impartial, but mainly because when I worked at Radio Tay our mascot was Tay-Tay the panda. On outside broadcasts it fell to a lowly member of the production team to wear the panda outfit and glad-hand startled listeners. I usually avoided the horror but on a few occasions it was unavoidable. I have never, before or since, smelt anything as foul as the inside of that panda outfit. It would be less unpleasant to find yourself inside an actual panda.

A passionate man with a loud hailer is trying to reason with the crowds, most of whom, I fear, don't have English as a first, second or third language. He's extolling the virtues of veganism, informing them that it's healthy, there are delicious alternatives to dairy and meat, and you don't have to shop at health food stores. He wants just one person to pledge them-selves to veganism, right here beneath Eros. He cheerfully reasons and pleads for about ten minutes. 'Just one person . . . please. Just one . . . '

No one comes forward and I sense the poor man crack. Gone is the appeal to our better nature as human beings. 'I see. So you're happy to have 150 million animals needlessly slaughtered just so you can eat them, eh?'

Someone claps. My friend arrives and I escape from Eros's steps to those of John Buchan.

27 July–3 August

Who took Terry?

Our foul-mouthed celebrity mascot has vanished

Terry the Turtle is missing. Sorry to be so blunt. I toyed with leading up to that statement, or finding less distressing words, or putting it into a foreign language (Google says this is the phrase in Lithuanian: 'Kilpiniai vėžlys nėra'), but I know most readers don't like to have things sugar-coated (except for a Mr The Tiger, who tells me he loves sugar-coating. Thanks for the email, Tony. You're great too.)

A few weeks ago Terry the Turtle was put in a drawer for the Queen's visit to Broadcasting House. There had been some concern that the green plastic motion-activated swearing machine might prove an ugly distraction on what was supposed to be a joyous occasion. Nobody wants a foul-mouthed reptilian tirade within earshot of the monarch.

Terry had his photo published in *Radio Times*, and as a result I noticed an increase in the number of people stopping by the *PM* desk to press his little button and get him to say the most appalling things. One person in particular was almost late for his slot on *Today*, giggling with naughty excitement as Terry poured forth with his expletive-filled monologue. 'Donkey ****', '***wipe' and 'big sweaty *****' were just three of the phrases that caused immense delight. In the end I had to say to the guy, 'Look, Archbishop, *Thought for the Day* is on in a minute – they're going to need you in studio.'

Terry was – and one does so hate to use this word – a celebrity. An unusual celebrity, yes. Plastic, shiny and no use without batteries inside him, but let's be honest, you could say the same about me.

Did I use the past tense just now to describe Terry? I fear I did. Here's what happened. The Monday after Terry appeared in *Radio Times*, I came into work at my usual time and sat at my desk waiting for someone to tell me what to do. At first there didn't seem to be anything unusual about the scene in front of me. Producers were bellowing into phones trying to persuade potential guests to turn themselves into actual guests. The editor was weeping quietly. And my own desk was festooned as always with flowers and letters of congratulation. I don't know why I keep sending them. I think they cheer me up.

'Something's missing,' I declared. The editor put down her balsam-infused tissue and said, 'No, Eddie, we've been through this. You haven't had a co-presenter since 2003. No one will work with you.'

'It's not that,' I sniffed. 'Terry the Turtle is missing.' He had indeed vanished from his usual desktop. I was all for calling the network and telling them we'd have to cancel *PM* to allow for a full search party, but someone pointed out there's no one at the Network Centre after four-thirty.

Days have passed. We've put up a sign appealing for his return, and police have cordoned the place off as a crime scene but candidly I fear the worst. I think his new-found celebrity resulted in him becoming yet another kidnapped plastic turtle. Or perhaps the first. Who honestly cares?

I will keep you posted. As Terry was fond of saying, '****'.

10–19 August

Turtle recall

I'm shell-shocked by Terry's reappearance

My thanks to all the kind readers who have enquired about Terry the Turtle.

Terry was a green plastic toy who sat on the shelf next to my desk at *PM* . . . sharing the space with a clutch of Sony awards and a pile of legal writs relating to stupid things I've said on air. Terry's USP was his ability to utter the vilest phrases with the push of a little black button on his chest or, depending on his motion-sensor settings, whenever someone walked past.

Terry rose to national prominence when he was removed from public view and put in a drawer as a precaution shortly before a visit to Broadcasting House by Her Majesty the Queen. There was some concern at the highest levels of the Corporation that, after its recent travails, if a robotic turtle was heard to call the Head of State a 'b***h' as she went about her business, the BBC would have to be shut down instantly. And rightly so.

A few days later, Terry went missing. His settings were motion sensor on/off and language PG/18+. There was no walkabout setting. He did not wander off. Someone stole him.

My calls to Scotland Yard were met with increasing impatience. Nick Ross didn't return my voicemails. Even a public appeal did not result in Terry's safe return.

By this point, I know you are dabbing tears of sympathy (or boredom) with a scented tissue, and I thank you for your concern. I would love to report a happy ending with perhaps an accompanying photo of me hugging Terry on the cover of *Radio Times*. Sadly, I can't report such a reunion, and as usual the editor hasn't returned my voicemails. What I can reveal is that there are some nice people out there.

I arrived at the *PM* office last week to see the familiar sights: Martha Kearney toiling away on *The World at One*; and someone in a sharp suit from the seventh floor wandering around with a clipboard, no doubt collecting material for his lunchtime seminar: 'How we can save money at the BBC by employing fewer producers by having more seminars like this one'. And wait – what's this? Yes there, in his familiar position: Terry the Turtle. Shiny, plastic and – let me press the button on his chest – 'b******s' – yes, sweary as ever. I let out a cheer of happiness, and the man with the clipboard scowls and makes another note.

Someone – some kind soul in our office – has bought a new Terry. The original had a missing eyebrow (don't ask), so I know this pristine turtle is a replacement. But in every other respect, Terry is back. His vocabulary is just the same. His facial expression, frozen in shock at his own bad language, is just the same.

I've asked around to find out who is responsible for this generous gesture, but no one is owning up. And so it is the kindness of a stranger.

Sometimes I look at the new Terry and miss the old one – like when you buy a puppy to replace a much-missed old stager. Sometimes I just marvel at the act of kindness that brought the new Terry into my life. And sometimes I look at him and think that maybe I should be getting on with my work.

14–20 September

The future is here

James Burke's seen 2053 – and it's tiny

The first three months of 1973 were taken up with the UK entering the EEC, IRA bombs going off in London, and Pink Floyd releasing *The Dark Side of the Moon*. Legal commercial radio wasn't yet born.

But on the cover of *Radio Times* (3–9 March, price 5p!), a sombre-looking James Burke was pondering something far removed from the everyday concerns of the early seventies. Through those sturdy glasses of his, James was looking to a future twenty years hence – 1993.

I know all this thanks to a whizzy new piece of internal BBC kit that allows staff to browse every cover and page of *Radio Times* going back to volume 1, number 1. Lighting upon Mr Burke, I delved in to see what he was predicting for 1993. And there, in an article written by Anthony Peagam, lay James's spookily accurate predictions.

Children growing up using technology to control their own lives better than anyone has done before. Computer-aided learning systems in schools, ending the days of chalk-and-talk. As traffic grows worse, controls may be set on private cars in urban areas. Smaller, 'clean' vehicles. The storage of personal information in data banks, with safeguards built in to protect against careless publication. It will be socially acceptable to take a pill to boost you through your day. The British people will reject identity cards. Computers in factories and offices everywhere.

I was eight in 1973 and my main worry then, as now, was whether I'd put my trousers on the right way. But I doubt many sentient adults were thinking the way Mr Burke was thinking and, of those, how many would be so correct?

I wondered what the great man was thinking now, in 2013, about life in the future. And so, a few days later, James Burke was sitting in the *PM* studio answering brilliantly and insightfully my lame questions. He had lots to say about internet privacy, what food people buy when they think a hurricane's coming, and how he'd slightly underestimated the prevalence of computers.

Then he began to talk about life in 2053. Here's my summary: something is going to happen in about forty years' time that will change things probably more than since we left the caves. Right now, in fourteen thousand laboratories around the world, nano-technology (the manipulation of matter on a very small scale) is making progress. In about forty years we might be able to have personal nano-factories. We could all make anything we want from air, dirt, water and a little acetylene gas ... 'the *Mona Lisa*, a piece of gold, a bottle of chardonnay'. We would all become autonomous. No need to live in cities. No need for governments or nation states.

For the whole interview search online for James Burke and Audioboo. I urge you to give it a listen. The great communicator has lost none of his power. And I urge any radio or TV people to consider the question so many listeners asked us when they heard the interview: why doesn't someone give this man his own show again? I've no idea whether he would want one, but wouldn't it be great?

21–27 September

My printer hell

James Burke's vision of 2053 has one fatal flaw . . .

Last week I regaled you with news of my encounter with James Burke, and how, back in 1973, Mr Burke had correctly predicted how our lives would change. In my recent interview with him, he cast his eyes forty years ahead to a world where nano-technology renders humans autonomous, without a need for governments or nation states. With a kind of souped-up 3D printer we will be able to create literally anything in our own homes. It was a mind-boggling few minutes.

This week I want to bring you a little of the background detail of what went on in the *PM* office shortly before the great scientist and futurologist arrived to record his interview foretelling human mastery of technology.

Me (to Amanda, top *PM* editor-type): 'Amanda, I want to print off that 1973 *Radio Times* cover to show to James. Do you think I can just print it on the normal printer?'

Amanda: 'Yes, darling.' (Amanda and I are not romantically involved. She calls everyone darling. She also seems to know a lot about how things work, which is why I'm asking her.) To my surprise, I successfully print the page.

Me, triumphantly: 'I've done it!'

Amanda: 'But it's in black and white, darling. Don't you want it in colour?'

Me: 'Does that printer print in colour?'

Amanda: 'No, darling, you need the Big Printer next to the bins.' (Several minutes pass while Amanda describes how to find the Big Printer, which it turns out has been hiding in plain sight ten yards away. Several more minutes pass while I locate the Big Printer on my computer screen, and then, with a flourish, press a button to make it print my page in colour. I make my way to the Big Printer and wait for it to do its colourful thing. One minute later I am back at Amanda's desk.

Me: 'It's broken. It says I need some kind of code. I mean, what's the point?'

Amanda, smiling but with a hint of weariness: 'Did you use your pass, darling? All the Big Printers need a BBC pass before they'll work.'

I repeat the computer print command then rush excitedly to the Big Printer, this time brandishing my pass. There's an error code.

Me (back at Amanda's desk): 'Amanda, it's not working. The technology in this place is *hopeless*.' (This accompanied by a certain amount of foot-stamping. They're used to it.)

Amanda, with the air of a woman who knew all along that this moment would come: 'Shall I try to print it for you, darling?'

Me, simpering: 'Would you?'

Moments later, I'm clutching a full-colour print of James Burke's 1973 *RT* cover, after a process that took a full fifteen minutes and involved no useful action by me. Without Amanda's expertise, I would have beaten my fists to a pulp on the Big Printer, and sobbed. Still. All's well that ends well.

At ten to three, Mr Burke himself arrives in the office. I introduce myself and, with some nervous excitement, ask if he'd like to see – in colour – the actual *RT* front cover from all those years ago.

JB: 'No, it's fine, thanks. I saw it online.'

28 September–4 October

Make mine a decaf

My name's Eddie – I'm addicted to coffee

Want to know what it feels like to be ninety? Give up caffeine. I recently found myself lying to a health professional who had asked me how many espressos I drank per day. She was looking at a chart, on a clipboard, the way health professionals do, and her pained facial expression indicated she really wanted to hear a nice low number of espressos per day. I resolved to give her the nice number she craved. Why make the poor woman's day worse? Sometimes lying is the right thing to do.

'Five,' I heard myself say.

She gasped and gave me a look that told me I should have chosen a lower number. '*Five?*' she enquired, in a pitch that Neil Sedaka himself could not have achieved. I decided the best course of action was to bluff it out.

'Yes', I said confidently. 'Four or five.'

This woman did not know that I have four or five before I leave the house in the morning, try to grab a double en route to the office, then chug heavily caffeinated drinks non-stop all day until 6 p.m. How could she? It crossed my mind that perhaps something on her clipboarded chart revealed the truth. I looked into her eyes to see whether she was buying what I hoped was an innocent expression.

Her lips were saying, 'Fine, Mr Mair, I'll put down five,' but her eyes were saying, 'Don't listen to my lips, they're lying. Like you. Bitch.' (I think she watches a lot of *Breaking Bad*.)

On my way back to the office, I considered all this over

a strong non-latte non-milky non-means-non double espresso. It was a moment of truth for me. 'Am I addicted to caffeine?'

Everyone in the coffee shop turned round, and I asked the question again, this time to myself. I drained the tiny cup of its hot, steaming, life-giving nectar and licked the lid, then the coffee ring on the table for the last vestiges of high.

I decided there was no way I was addicted and to prove it to myself I decided I would come off caffeine once and for all. How hard could it be?

At home for the next fortnight, I ran down my stocks of lovely caffeinated beverages and began to stock up on their decaf alternatives. They even looked less interesting. But I wasn't letting that put me off. When I set my mind to achieve something, I do not rest until I achieve it. Or at least until something brightly coloured or sparkly distracts me.

Yesterday morning, I had the last of my regular coffee and then left the country on holiday. I figured it would be a good idea to face my coffee demons while relaxed in the sunshine rather than at work. I would hate my colleagues to catch even a glimpse of me as an angry, self-centred, thoughtless git who treated them badly. Especially with those tribunals looming.

So here I am, writing to you. Thirty-six hours caffeine-free. A headache that began yesterday afternoon – a really satisfying dull thud – is banging along now. I have just been for a nap in the middle of the afternoon and life seems a lot drearier than it used to.

I will let you know of my progress. For now: this must be what ninety feels like.

16–22 November

Exhibit A – me!

My day as a National Trust landmark

Life should be full of new experiences no matter your vintage, and I am pleased to report that last week I was, for the very first time, an exhibit in a National Trust home.

For years on *PM* we have marked the glory of autumn by sending a radio car to Stourhead in Wiltshire where the head gardener, Alan Power, casts his eye over the vista and describes it most lyrically for eager listeners. You have to hear him to believe it.

Just as many people feel Christmas hasn't begun until they've heard the carols at King's, or that the election campaign hasn't begun until some politician lambasts the BBC, I don't believe it's autumn until Alan Power has described it for me.

This year we decided to go one step further: take the programme on the road and broadcast the whole hour live from Stourhead.

It's a complicated business. An engineer has to make the journey several weeks before to pick a suitable broadcast point, and liaise with the venue to ensure everything we need is available. This ranges from power points through WiFi to my demands for a fully stocked mini-bar (NO mini-Toblerone, thank you).

Producers then get to work fixing guests and planning how the hour will work. This is more arduous for a news programme than, say, *Woman's Hour*. We can have prepared the most scintillating hour of outside broadcast, but if a big news event happens we must cancel all our plans and give the event our full attention.

Cutbacks mean life on the road is less glamorous than in days gone by. While previously I would have been whisked to an OB venue in the BBC Learjet, that's had to be sold off to pay for another internal BBC inquiry into extravagant spending. I found myself at 5 a.m. standing by the on ramp to the M3, holding up a sign saying: 'Wiltshire or nearby?' I'm ashamed to admit I only got a lift by flashing a bit of leg. Organic leg of lamb, which always gets me a lift from hungry truckers willing to swap free-range for a free ride.

Arriving at Stourhead, Alan was there to greet me and we set off on what I can only describe as a magical morning. The gardens are hilariously beautiful. Alan's knowledge and passion heightened the experience to the point where, at times, I had tears in my eyes. And we were there before the place was open to the public. I felt like the Beckhams must do when shops open exclusively for them. Only I was wearing better aftershave.

We made our way back to the entrance hall of the main house that would serve as our studio once it closed to visitors at 4 p.m. Until then, we worked in a room at the back of the hall – fully visible to visitors but roped off, like a VIP area, or a crime scene.

They would come in the grand entrance and survey the majesty of the room. Then their eyes would alight on three BBC people hunched over laptops, agitatedly trying to get the WiFi to work. Most would blink, a little confused by the anachronism, and move on to the next room, wondering privately what was going wrong with the National Trust. Only one woman asked if I was Eddie Mair from *PM*. She said she was a big fan. So we had her sectioned.

7–13 December

I talk rubbish

Ever get a terrible case of foot-in-mouth disease?

Heard on Radio 4 the other week, an earnest trailer for a tension-filled drama. Here's what the script said:

> Man: 'What makes a man kill?'
> Woman: 'Weekday afternoons on BBC Radio 4 . . .'

And you can't really argue with that. I'm sure the trailer people didn't spot the juxtaposition and I'm in no position to criticise. My ability to disconnect my brain from my mouth live on air can be heard nightly – and, worse than that, I've taken to writing howlers in advance into my own scripts.

Recently we did an item on *PM* about the variable form of the Manchester City and England goalkeeper Joe Hart. As usual I wrote my script into our computerised running order during the afternoon, for me to blurt out on the programme. I wrote: 'Spare a thought, then, for Joe Hart. He's the goalkeeper for Manchester United and England who has hit a run of bad form, making mistakes for his team and his country.'

Did you spot my mistake? Thankfully a young producer went into the script before transmission and changed United to City: 'We're here to spare your blushes, Eddie.' The script on the page that I would read on air was correct, no thanks to me. Buffoon.

And the story would end there – except here is what I said live on *PM* to squillions of listeners: 'Spare a thought, then, for Joe Hart. He's the goalkeeper for Manchester United and

England who has hit a run of bad form, making mistakes for his team and his country.'

Yes, something in my brain just wanted me to say United. I know Joe plays for City – I've watched him on the telly. At no stage did I associate him with the red team. The word on the page was City, yet the word that came tumbling out of my mouth was unquestionably United.

Here I was casting doubt on the talents of a gifted professional who sometimes made mistakes in the heat of the moment, yet I couldn't stop myself from screwing up, despite preparing in advance, having my work checked by a more alert colleague, and with the correct words written clearly in front of me. Doctors have a word for this; the word is stupidity.

I wish I could tell you this is an isolated example but sadly it isn't. Would you like to hear another gem from the Eddie Mair Archive of Unmitigated Rubbish? Here is something else I wrote in a script recently and read out on air: 'They're invariably wrong. But sometimes, just sometimes, they're right.'

The good people at Collins advise this on the word 'invariably': 'Adverb: always; without exception'. Just to drive the point home they add that it means 'regularly, constantly, every time, inevitably, repeatedly, consistently, continually, eternally, habitually, perpetually, customarily, unfailingly, on every occasion, unceasingly, twenty-four-seven, day in, day out'.

So you see, 'sometimes, just sometimes, they're right' doesn't really enter into it. I just thank my lucky stars Sir Alex Ferguson is no longer in charge or I'd be on the receiving end of one of those famous 'hairdryer' rants that he invariably sometimes gave.

14–20 December

Ask me about parking!

I'm embracing the traffic warden community

It's unusual, I know, to have sympathy for traffic wardens – but spare a thought for the poor souls tramping the streets of Westminster. They seem lumbered with more equipment than a determined mountaineer halfway up K2.

Now I've noticed that in addition to all the usual gubbins they have a large friendly sign on the front of their sturdy jackets that says 'Ask Me About Parking'. When I first saw an attendant wearing one, I assumed he was an over-enthusiastic loner who would be mercilessly ribbed by colleagues in the Traffic Warden Canteen (ample free parking). But then I saw others sporting the same sign.

What could it mean? Most people encounter traffic wardens at that critical nexus where the warden's arrival and your allotted parking time have missed each other by seconds. Why would you want to ask them about parking then? At that moment, when a parking attendant is photographing your car as though there were three headless corpses in the back, a chat about what single and double yellows mean on a Saturday afternoon is the furthest thing from your mind.

I assume it's a well-intentioned PR manoeuvre to change our perceptions of the humble traffic warden/parking attendant/who knows what they're called now. Parking Ambassadors? Traffic Czars? Self-Driven Vehicle Space Accessibility Specialists? No longer seen as the scourge of the motorist, they are your friend: keeping traffic moving and making sure hard-working families can park their hard-working cars on the hard-working streets.

After several days of seeing these jackets demanding that I ask a warden about parking, I finally did. The poor man was struggling up Great Portland Street – past the ghost of Kenneth Williams – knees buckling under the weight of his enormous jacket. I tapped him on the shoulder in as friendly a way as I could and nodded towards the message on his chest.

'Excuse me,' I beamed. 'Would you mind if I asked you about parking?'

He was a little startled, no doubt instantly recognising my voice and wondering what to say when confronted with a broadcasting titan. He managed to blurt out, 'No, go ahead, Eamonn.'

And so I went for it: 'I was wondering if you had any advice on parallel parking. Mine stinks. Most of my efforts end up on YouTube.' He said he couldn't really help me with that. So I tried something else.

'Is it better to drive round and round a supermarket car park for a space near the store, or should you save petrol by parking in the big empty spaces near the recycling bins?'

He said he couldn't really help me with that. So I tried something else. 'What's the story with single and double yellows on Saturdays?'

He replied: 'Single and double yellow lines indicate that parking restrictions are in place and no waiting is allowed. You can park on single yellow lines outside the hours of control, but you cannot park on double yellow lines at any time. In some areas, the hours of control on single yellow lines end at 1.30 p.m. on a Saturday.'

2014

The joy of stairs

How to avoid the BBC's busiest people

Fergus Walsh, the BBC's medical correspondent, wrote recently that he never uses the lifts in New Broadcasting House. He resolved to always take the stairs for two reasons: one, it's healthier; and two, he's too impatient to wait for the lift.

Good for Fergus, I say – it's a fine example to us all. But new year or no, I will not be resolving to follow in his footsteps. I'd like to, but there are a *lot* of storeys. For me, a walk from the *Newsnight* studio on −3 to the top floor, where I think the director-general has his own private lair, would in all likelihood cause me to lose consciousness – and not just from the whiff of the D-G's cologne.

Then there is the problem of the spiral staircases in New BH. Like all spiral staircases, they are easy on the eye and crying out for someone in a ball gown to sweep down them majestically, but they are murder if you fail to concentrate while negotiating them. The narrow bits can be very dicey if your feet are anything over a size 8. If everyone at the BBC took the stairs instead of the lift, there would be a calamity.

I shudder to think of the headlines if I was crushed to death under a pile of collapsing correspondents. John Simpson would never forgive himself.

The upside of using the stairs would be the joy of avoiding some of the BBC's BUSIEST people. They are the ones who are so monstrously busy they can't just get in the lift and wait for the doors to close. Oh no. They *must* push the little button that forces the doors shut at their behest.

It's the oddest thing. I see them alongside me, waiting for the lift to arrive for sometimes a full two or three minutes. There is much shuffling of feet and looking at watches as if the process of waiting might make them ill – yet they're not in such a hurry they take the stairs.

When the lift arrives, their sense of urgency becomes overwhelming. They might have waited for minutes on end for the lift, but the thought of waiting a further five seconds to allow the door to close automatically sends them into finger-jabbing paroxysms. They lunge at the little 'door close' button and stab at it ferociously until the doors glide to a satisfying close. Invariably, they get off after one floor.

I've tried to consider what would make people do this. An obvious answer is that they don't want to be in a lift with me for a second longer than necessary, and I can't really argue with that. Or perhaps they like to have a little control over the lift, which generally seems to have a mind of its own. Maybe they're just properly busy in a way I can't understand.

But this mad sense of urgency is not confined to the BBC. In hotels around the world I've encountered the same frantic finger-stabbing. Even at resorts where the only thing people have to worry about is where to get their next cocktail, I've witnessed the desperate lunge for that little button.

We're all in such a hurry. Why? I call upon lift-makers to do away with the door-close button. What do you say,

Schindler's Lifts? Come on, Otis Elevator Company, why not?

Let's enjoy the leisurely door-close, and to hell with the rush.

11–17 January

Hi, I'm Eggie!

But you can call me Anastasia

Hello. I want you to be among the first to know that I'm changing my identity. In future I will be known as . . . Eddie Mair. I realise this won't come as a shock to you, but I'd like to explain my thinking.

Initially I toyed with the idea of changing my name to Anastasia Beaverhausen or General Sir Anthony Cecil Hogmanay Melchett, because they would render my life more colourful.

'Good evening, this is *PM* with Anastasia Beaverhausen.' Or 'Good evening, this is *PM* with General Sir Anthony Cecil Hogmanay Melchett. Sir Anthony is off tonight, I'm Carolyn Quinn.' Endless fun. Lovers of situation comedy will know the names are already associated with other people – Karen Walker from *Will & Grace*, and the pigeon-loving great survivor from *Blackadder Goes Forth* – so they're probably off-limits to me. The same goes for Lulu.

Why am I changing my name? It all started when I switched mobile phone company to a new network that insists on the chattiest of correspondence. All the bills, emails and texts greet me by my first name, like an old pal putting their arm around my shoulder after several pints. I don't really mind this, except the name they have for me is from the credit card I used to join them: Edward.

This name has been handed down a few generations, but like my uncle and grandfather before me, I've never been called that by anyone. It's been Eddie for as long as I can remember, apart from, I'm told, in my earliest years when I referred to myself as Eggie. Stupid boy.

After the umpteenth text arrived from my chummy mobile network I decided to ask if they wouldn't mind just abbreviating the Edward to Eddie. The people at the call centre told me that was impossible. I explained I wasn't trying to change my last name, or change my first name to Anastasia. It was just like Robert becoming Bob or Elizabeth becoming Liz. I think they thought I was a complete Richard.

They explained they could only change the name over the phone if Edward had been a typo. To change the name, I would need to write.

Two months later a letter arrived addressed to Edward, explaining that they would also need some documentation, such as a driving licence or passport. Fair enough: identity theft is serious. But it turns out that to get your driving licence changed they need to see a passport with your new name. Or vice versa. Baaaah, I thought. If it's going to be this hard I might as well go for a name with Hogmanay in it.

After several pints with friends, who had already forgotten my name anyway, I resolved to see this through to the end. The passport people had explained that by legally changing my name by deed poll (or wait a minute . . . why not change it *to* Deed Poll?) all the paperwork would fall into place.

I called my solicitor, who advised that the whole thing would only cost a few hundred pounds! What a marvellous use of money.

As I write I await the paperwork. It is my fervent hope

that before long, you will be able to call me Eddie Mair. Although I'm a bit worried I wrote Eggie on the form. I'll say it was a typo.

18–24 January

Oi! Stop texting

Why are we all glued to our mobiles?

I was called a paedo recently. Not unusual for a broadcaster in this day and age, I suppose, but the woman who made the accusation had literally just bumped into me.

I saw her from a distance. She was walking towards me, mesmerised by her mobile phone. Perhaps she'd just tweeted something delightful, or was checking a Nigella recipe. It may be that she was looking at a map. One thing for sure is that she wasn't looking where she was going. She was fairly barrelling down the street but at no stage did she look up.

As she got closer, I surmised that she might have been a little drunk. Certainly she was unkempt. Had we been on a bus she would undoubtedly have chosen to sit next to me.

I resolved to do my best to steer clear of her. This proved tricky as no matter how much I tried to avoid her uncertain gait, she continued to weave in my direction. She got closer and closer, her eyes still locked on her mobile. I made one final attempt to get out of her way but the inevitable happened. Unlike two ships passing in the night, we collided.

Any hopes I'd harboured that the silly ninny would apologise for not looking where she was going were cruelly shattered by her cry of 'Oi! What the eff do you think you're doing?'

I resolved to keep walking rather than get involved in an ugly confrontation. Did I mention she was ugly? As I strode away, she continued yelling at my back. Perhaps she'd been checking sweary websites on her mobile because she had a choice collection of four-letter words, which she hurled at me in order to get me to turn around. I kept walking until it must have been clear even to the yelling dimwit that I wasn't for turning. It's at this point that she began to yell 'paedo' at me.

Part of me wanted to go and physically remonstrate with the woman but I knew that morally it was almost certainly the wrong thing to do. Plus she would probably thrash me in a fight. I considered going back and taking a photograph of the wild-haired loon and tweeting it, but again that was almost certainly the wrong thing to do.

In the end I resolved to do what all decent people should do when faced with a situation like that: get back at the festering old troll by writing about her in *Radio Times*.

I doubt very much that she will read this, but on the off-chance she does, let me say this directly to her: you are a rude, boorish, hideous woman, and I hope you lose even more of your teeth.

I feel a lot better for that, thank you.

She is an extreme example of a growing trend: people striding down the street transfixed by their mobiles. I think the rest of us are just supposed to throw ourselves out of their way. It's a provocative action, to wilfully put your own desperate need to walk 'n' text ahead of everyone else. Are they really so busy they can't stop for a second?

It's not just texting. I've seen people reading ebooks while walking down busy streets. And you know what's even worse? I've been known to walk 'n' text, too, making me a hypocrite as well as a pavement lout. It makes me want to physically remonstrate with myself.

1–7 February

Last post

Will my funeral deserve a five-star rating?

A day off *PM* to attend the funeral of a friend. The persistent cough turned out to be stage-four lung cancer. Life's everyday cruelty leaves a family bewildered. My sadness nothing compared to their pain.

It's 2014, so news of the funeral location arrived in a text message and, being the modern man I am, I went online to search for the location of the crematorium. Not yet being at the age where all I do is attend funerals, this felt a strange thing to be doing. As with all of death's rituals, what is extraordinary for us when we occasionally bump up against them is an everyday occurrence for those in the business.

This would explain why the crematorium had its own website. Its own website! I don't know why this shocked me. In fact, it was extremely helpful. Opening hours, parking information, details of nearest bus stops and Tube stations. A map of the grounds and gardens, and guides for the bereaved on the crematorium's procedures for flowers, music and the hushed question of ashes. You can even take a virtual tour of the place. I decided not to, in order to leave some mystery for the day itself.

Better than that, my Google search turned up two reviews of the place! In the style of TripAdvisor or *The Good Food*

Guide, you can now compare how Britain's crematoriums stack up.

I did wonder whether crematorium complainants would be extraordinarily picky. 'An otherwise excellent funeral was *ruined* because the curtains closed fractionally too slowly.' 'Pew legroom disappointing.' 'Deathly quiet.'

Perhaps in the style of authors who secretly go online to big up their latest work, people in the death business do the same. 'Another *excellent* funeral at the Acme Cremmy. I cannot wait for my own demise so I can fully enjoy all their facilities.' 'Superb service. I laughed, I cried, I nearly died.'

Happily the two reviewers each gave this particular crematorium five stars. I would too, though is it fair to judge on one visit? I'll maybe pop back next year to be sure.

Breaking bad

'8.56 p.m. Lionel's enjoying some alone time,' intoned Marcus Bentley, wickedly, on a recent episode of *Celebrity Big Brother*. We see the great Lionel Blair relaxing in the garden, away from his housemates. There is a glass of wine on the table, cigarette in his hand. Then we hear the beloved star of *Give Us a Clue* and a million tap-dance routines exclaim 'Oh!' before he lifts one buttock off the sofa to let rip with a wind-break that literally leaves him breathless. Like a hundred-metre dash, the whole thing is over in about ten seconds, but it was probably the highlight of the series. Do look for it on YouTube. It's matched only by the moment a very angry Lionel yelled at Big Brother down an angry red telephone. It was like seeing the Queen Mother swear.

Guilt trip

A Catholic friend of mine informs me of a recent change at his local church. It has long been a tradition that a list of church-goers who are unwell is posted at the door, in order that people can include the names of the sick in prayers. No more. Apparently the list might breach the Data Protection Act.

22–23 February

Inside the Beeb

I meet, therefore I am (in a meeting)

New Broadcasting House has a New System for Having Meetings. As you can imagine, this is a fantastically important development, because at the BBC we like to have meetings. Our priorities are very clear. They are printed on the back of every BBC ID card.

The words might as well be imprinted on my heart because I can recite them for you here without even consulting my card. They are about BBC Values and what we stand for:

1. Try to have a meeting.
2. If you're not having a meeting you should be planning one.
3. If you're not having or planning a meeting you should be talking to someone about the pointlessness of your last meeting.

4. Actually I'm a bit vague on this one. Something about educate and inform?
5. If you are unable to have, plan or talk about a meeting, and there are no other options, make a programme.

For the past few weeks an exciting new electronic room-booking system has been in place. Every meeting room must be booked online in advance. You enter a room by holding your ID card against a screen. If the light stays yellow, you cannot enter. If it turns red, you may pass! It's a perfectly fine system let down by the buffoons who can't use it. By which I mean me.

I acknowledge that I do not know how to set the out-of-office autoreply on my email, or which hand of the director-general to kiss first. But I'd hoped I could manage the new system. Yet most days at 11 a.m. or 2.45 p.m. you can see me trying to gain entry to a *PM* meeting, point-lessly holding my card against the little screen only to have it reject me every time. I must rely on the kindness of strangers to go to my own meetings. A colleague tells me my ID card might have to be reprogrammed, though the look in her eyes suggested she thought I might benefit from a digital overhaul.

Wrong place, wrong person

A friend tells me of a funeral she attended. Like me, she only knew the deceased, not the family, and solemnly trooped in to pay her respects. After a burst of 'The Lord is my Shepherd', as the congregation held back tears, the minister intoned that it was indeed a sad day for everyone who knew Brian Davidson.

Sadly my friend had gone not for Brian but for Lily. It was an extra sad day for her because she was at the wrong funeral. Lily would not be formally mourned for another week.

What would you do? Classily, my friend stayed and grieved for whoever Brian was, but dashed out the second the ceremony was over. She felt bad about even that because by all accounts Brian was a lovely man.

Twenty fourteen

In a future edition of *RT*: why did one *Newsnight* presenter secretly complain about a colleague's legs? Which BBC boss got into trouble for going to Umbria? Why does Frankie Howerd dominate top-level meetings at Broadcasting House? And why does his ID card work but mine doesn't? I'll be reporting from the set of *Twenty Twelve* spin-off *W1A*, set in the heart of the BBC.

1–7 March

Runt of the litter

There's always one on a panel show

A top BBC executive says, 'We're not going to have panel shows on any more with no women on them.' I'm not going to get involved in that discussion. It's the kind of thing only top BBC executives should have to worry about, like whether a rival executive has a nicer office or how they're going to placate the ten presenters to whom they've privately promised one job.

My rule would be: 'We're not going to have panel shows on any more with one duff contestant on them.' You know how it works. Your favourite panel show has two team captains and two or four more participants. They all sparkle and shine except for one: the runt of the litter, who is almost edited out of the show. You can see them in the opening credits smiling winningly and waving like a ninny; twenty-eight minutes later they are husks: dead eyes simultaneously pleading for a cyanide capsule and their agent's mobile number.

Only one of their contributions survives the edit. It can be seen about ten minutes into the show. A mildly amusing remark meets with an almost imperceptible chortle from a lone audience member. Fellow panellists fix supportive grins but they know from years of roaming the wild comedy circuit that this wildebeest will be dog food before the edit is over.

I know because I have been that wildebeest.

Many years ago I was asked to appear on Radio 4's *The News Quiz*. They should have renamed it *The Gnus Quiz* that night. The huge sense of honour I felt at being asked gave way on the evening of the recording to a crushing sense of inadequacy and fear that I usually only get when I walk into any room.

Simon Hoggart was in charge (and how much we miss his writing and broadcasting today) with Alan Coren (ditto) and Jeremy Hardy (thank goodness, still going). Right there you have three of the sharpest, most experienced wits in the land. And me. It's one thing to raise a weak smile on the radio with a faintly funny remark as you hand to the weather. Quite another to be able to survey the week's news and make people roar with laughter with a mix of devastating bombast, sly asides, brilliant flights of fancy and sizzling satire.

I remember very little about what I said that night, and

I'm sure I'm not alone in that. My abiding memory is of sitting next to Mr Hardy (I was not resting on my Laurels) in a state of wonder. I'd heard him on the radio many times, but to be at his side while he held forth and improvised with such energy for minutes at a time, making the audience giggle or guffaw with almost every sentence ... that was awe-inspiring.

Years passed before I agreed to do anything like that again, on a new comedy panel show for Sky. I only agreed to do it because I knew the pilot would never be broadcast. But as the recording began, I was instantly transported back to the dark memory of my *News Quiz* recording. Here I was, having agreed to appear on the same show as Lee Mack, David Walliams and Jimmy Carr. What was I thinking? I was not asked back when the series was commissioned, and quite right too.

Should you ever see or hear me appearing as the spare wheel on a panel show, feel free to shove this *Radio Times* article in my face.

Comedy, like surgery, should be left to the professionals.

8–14 March

Gone fishing

I'm yet to master the out-of-office email

I am away from the office this week, though you would never know it from the lack of out-of-office autoreply on my emails. I once emailed a journalist on a national newspaper and got this out of office reply: 'Sorry, I am out of the office writing a book. I will be back when it's finished.'

Casting round colleagues for opinions, there was division. About half considered him the most pretentious tool in the box, while the other half marvelled at his determination to up sticks and leave the demands of the office behind: he might as well have written 'Gone fishin''.

The out-of-office autoreply is the email equivalent of the closed office door, or the unanswered telephone. Despite myself, I scan the reply for hints that I may, after all, be loved.

Some are as brutal as Mr Gone Fishin'. They baldly state they are not in the office between these dates (translation: to hell with you). An even more detached version of this is the reply that carries no dates, just the email address of someone else in the office (translation: to hell with all of you). I respect these people.

Others offer tantalising hope that the apparently closed door might be ajar, that the phone might be answered: 'I am out of the office until Friday but I hope to check periodically for urgent emails.' Bingo! This person *might* get back in touch. You *might* get a second date. But wait: did my original email sound urgent enough? I have been known to go back and check. I respect these people.

I used to have a boss at the BBC who seemed to be on permanent out-of-office, even though I knew he was usually in his office. It would say: 'If it's urgent, call the mobile.' A nice touch – only people who really knew the man would have his mobile, so that reduced substantially the chance of him being troubled unnecessarily.

And it placed the burden of responsibility on the emailer. This boss is making himself available to you, but will probably demote you if you interrupt his important meeting with a phone call about paper clips. People like that I can work with. I respect these people.

And then there is the final category of out-of-office

autoreply: 'Sorry, I am not in the office right now. I have just stepped out to the coffee machine and will be back in seven or eight minutes depending on the queue and whether I have to change the filters. Then at lunchtime I'm out for a sandwich for twenty-eight minutes. From Friday I WILL be on holiday and completely uncontactable but will be checking emails half-hourly. I can also be contacted at the Marriott [he leaves the phone *and* fax number], or, if I have an accident, at one of these hospitals [he leaves the phone *and* fax numbers]. Best wishes, Brian, Deputy Assistant Head of Paper Clips.' I do not respect these people.

Does Brian ever really get a break? Will he ever get lost in a good book, or go scuba diving, or find love in an unexpected place? I fear he will only ever find true peace in the grave, where he will be buried with his BlackBerry, Samsung and iPhone, and a bag of golden paper clips.

'Sorry, I am dead. I can be contacted either in heaven [just the phone number – there are no faxes in heaven] or hell [just a fax number].'

Me? I never set an out-of-office autoreply because I don't know how to.

15–21 March

Ha, Hitler

I'd like to share a Mel Brooks anecdote

Is there a more electrifying moment in the history of cinema than the scene in *Network* when news anchor Howard Beale demands his viewers get up and yell out of their windows 'I'm as mad as hell and I'm not going to take this any more'?

I can tell you, from my less than encyclopaedic knowledge of films, that *Network* is a spellbinding, often hilarious satire on TV and TV news. Peter Finch won the Oscar, posthumously, for his portrayal of Howard Beale, the TV anchor who threatened to blow his brains out on air ... and whose ratings went through the roof.

On holiday last week I read a brilliant book about the film, written by Dave Itzkoff: *Mad as Hell*. It's a beautifully researched, well-written piece of work.

It's full of intimate details, making you feel like you were there when the film was shot. Itzkoff recounts Faye Dunaway's sex-scene anxiety. He knows the view from the office where Paddy Chayefsky wrote the screenplay. And he reveals that while Chayefsky was a stickler for the written word, when shooting the seminal scene Peter Finch inserted an extra 'as' into the original script (which called for him to say: 'I'm mad as hell ... ') – and got away with it.

So far, so nerdy, I suppose. You'd need to really love the film to buy the book. But there's another reason I mention it: it has a great Mel Brooks anecdote.

I love Mel Brooks more than a gentile should. Don't get me started. The beauty of his stated aim of making us all laugh at Adolf Hitler came home to me when I recently watched *Downfall*, a film about Hitler's final days in his bunker (by the way, check the alternative ending. Did not see THAT coming).

Every time Nazis in the film said 'Heil Hitler' to the Führer, I was reminded of Mel playing Hitler in *To Be or Not to Be*. Whenever his Nazis said 'Heil Hitler' to him, he would do a mini Nazi salute and say 'Heil myself'. And so there I was, giggling during *Downfall*. Thanks Mel.

Anyway, here's that anecdote. Picture it: midtown Manhattan, New York, 1969. The Carnegie Deli. Chayefsky is bemoaning the state of television with producer Howard Gottfried and Mel Brooks. He says TV execs wouldn't know whether *The Threepenny Opera* was written by Bertolt Brecht or Hy the plumber. They 'probably wouldn't know that Bertolt Brecht had been dead for years'.

'Leave it to me,' says Brooks, his eyes agleam. 'I'll call one of the networks.' He went to a phone booth, returning minutes later to report back.

He'd called NBC and asked for an executive. 'Hello dere,' Brooks had said. 'Dis is Berrrrrtolt Brrrrecht. I vaunted to talk about der TV rights to my musical *Der Thrrrrrreepenny Operrrra.*'

The secretary said she would put him through and placed the phone on the desk, so the sound from the office was still audible to Brooks.

Secretary: 'There's a Bertolt Brecht calling for you. Something about *The Threepenny Opera*?'
Executive: 'What are you talking about? Bertolt Brecht is dead!'
Secretary: 'How can Bertolt Brecht be dead? He's on the phone for you right now!'
Executive: 'Oh, well, that's different – put him on.'

22–28 March

Beep, beep, beep

Why I've had a lot of sleepless nights

Keen listeners to *PM* might have noticed that I was even more rubbishy than usual on the programme the other week. For that I would normally blame the producers, the editors, the weather or Nick Clegg (everybody blames him for everything), but it was none of those. My poor performance was caused by ... smoke alarms.

'A working smoke alarm is essential. It provides vital early warning and extra time to escape if there is a fire. Every home should have at least one working smoke alarm.' So says the website of the London Fire Brigade, and I want to make it absolutely clear that, regardless of what I'm about to say, I agree with every word of that, without equivocation. Smoke alarms save lives. Check yours now. And if you don't have a smoke alarm, please go and buy one.

That said, there were times this week when I wanted to smash all three of my smoke alarms to smithereens, then bury the smithereens in a shallow grave, dance on it, and commission a headstone that read 'Here lie three smashed-up smoke alarms. You're not beeping now, are you? Hahahahahaha.' I'll grant you, most monumental masons would baulk at that phrasing, and that many words would set me back a bob or two, but let me tell you it would be worth every penny.

I returned from holiday to find smoke alarm one chirping intermittently. Within moments I was teetering precariously on an inappropriate chair, changing the battery. The beeping stopped. I'm a domestic god, as you can imagine.

The next night, alarm number two was doing the same thing. See previous paragraph. It was alarm number three that was put on earth by Satan him/herself. In the middle of the night, it began to chirrup intermittently. As you might know, the beep of a smoke alarm has more decibels than Shirley Bassey struggling to be heard over the sound of an aircraft taking off from a packed Wembley Stadium.

I replaced the battery, but the satanic alarm was having none of it. I returned to bed to be woken by a full-blown siren. The alarm appeared to believe the house was an inferno. Back up on the chair at 3 a.m., I checked the wiring. The alarm is connected to the mains; the battery is a back-up. All seemed in order. The siren stopped.

Then started again an hour later.

The next two nights were carbon copies. If you're thinking, why didn't I remove the battery/disconnect the wiring/ turn it all off at the mains ...? I tried all that. IT STILL BEEPED! It was a *RoboCop* alarm.

Twenty-four hours a day it would choose to chirrup like a cricket, or wake the dead with its amusing siren noise. Bleary-eyed at 2 a.m. I checked what the internet had to offer. It turns out that around the world smoke alarms behave like wet gremlins. People resort to desperate measures to get away from the noise. They move house. They drive off cliffs. Others even watch Piers Morgan.

The internet taught me that all such alarms have a use-by date. I found one on the underside of the alarm at 1 a.m. Gosh, it was fun. I also discovered that dust can cause a malfunction.

I never imagined myself on a chair in the middle of the night, using the furry attachment to hoover a smoke alarm on the ceiling, but there I was. And it stopped the noise. Goodnight.

5–11 April

Let's get radical

My ten-point plan to shake up the BBC

There has been no shortage of advice recently on the future of the BBC. What services it should cut, whether not paying the TV licence fee should be a criminal offence and how the Corporation should be funded.

Much of the advice has come from people who took the BBC shilling for yonks, then five minutes after cashing their redundancy cheque publicly demanded the demolition of Broadcasting House. Tempting though it is to follow in their illustrious footsteps, I'm going to be even bolder and hold forth now with my blueprint for the future of the BBC. I believe it's a vision that the BBC's critics and supporters can rally around. You're welcome, Britain.

1. The plan to close BBC3 as a TV network doesn't go far enough. If the BBC is to show its commitment to radical change, I believe it will have to give up an entire letter of its name and become simply the BC: British Corporation.

2. Removing one B from the letterhead of BBC stationery will bring ink-cost savings of a hundred million pounds a year: enough to re-carpet the walls of Broadcasting House in dynamic colours that will inspire everyone to be even more creative.

3. Removing the word 'Broadcasting' from the BBC's name means the Corporation will reach the goal it's been working towards for many years. Currently, 89 per cent of jobs in the BBC have nothing to do with broadcasting. When the BC is established, the remaining 11 per cent can safely be moved from frontline services.

4. The BBC has already shown its commitment to reflecting the whole of Britain with its Salford initiative. I propose that the BC should go further, literally, by relocating everything to Unst, in the far north of the Shetland Islands.

5. Locating to the northernmost point in Britain will allow the BC to commit to its favourite thing: pandering to people in the south.

6. While the initial relocation costs will be high, and the building of a fifteen-storey gold-standard digital hub broadcasting centre in Muckle Flugga will startle local ponies, the long-term cost savings will be enough to re-carpet the walls of the broadcasting centre in new dynamic colours that will inspire everyone in television to be even more creative.

7. By relocating so close to Scandinavia, the BC will be able to broadcast shows like *The Bridge* and *The Killing* by hijacking the signal from across the North Sea. The long-term cost savings will be enough to re-carpet the walls etc.

8. In the event of Scottish independence, points 4–7 will be in jeopardy and I haven't really thought of a plan B.

9. I believe that non-payment of the TV licence fee should remain a criminal offence, but only if the BC is also held accountable for its programmes in a court of law. I'd do away with *Feedback* and *Points of View*, and allow licence-payers to bring criminal charges against programme-makers who make criminally bad programmes. Of course this would clog up the judicial system but by allowing the cameras in to record sentencing the BC *News at Six* would have terrific footage every night. Executives found guilty on more than three occasions will be put to death and the footage shown after the watershed in the BC *News at Ten*. They will not have their walls re-carpeted.

10. Ticket sales from the public executions will replace the licence fee.

19–25 April

It's a new age

The day I chose discounts over eternal youth

At a shop in upstate New York recently, I reached a milestone in my life.

At the checkout I had just delicately arranged all my proposed purchases: hundreds of dollars' worth of the finest wool/cashmere suits, silk ties and footwear so refined your feet were virtually guaranteed to hurt.

(Why am I lying to you? It was in fact a pile of cheap lumberjack shirts, absolutely no ties and a pair of comfy loafers so hideous that even a nurse wouldn't wear for them for a twelve-hour shift.)

The smiling, chatty, friendly American assistant was getting on my nerves. Unaware that I live in London, where conversations with strangers are confined to helping police with their enquiries or taking part in a vox pop, he was chirping away like I was his best friend. It was non-stop attentiveness.

In my heart, I knew the guilty party in this exchange was me, so I did my best to show willing by adopting the smile pioneered by Gordon Brown. The assistant asked if I needed to know where the restrooms were.

Again, sorry, I'm lying about that last bit. I think I'm trying to put off the awful moment when I have to share this story.

My rictus grin and occasional grunting were no match for the assistant's relentless happiness. Eventually, he totted up the cost of my spree and asked if I had a store card. I would get 15 per cent off if I had a store card.

In what may have been my first actual words since arriving at the till, I said I lived in the UK and didn't really have a need for one. As soon as the words were out of my mouth I realised my mistake. I had opened up a whole new avenue of conversation for my eager buddy to walk down.

After several more minutes in which he held forth on Princess Diana, British dentistry and the 'blaaaady weather' we arrived back at the point where he was asking for money.

'So,' he mused, staring at the till. 'We really must find a way to get you a discount.' I tried to protest but he was having none of it. He turned to look at me, with a flash of excitement in his eyes. He'd thought of something!

'I know! I can get you the Seniors' Discount! You're over fifty-five, yes?'

Across state lines in New Jersey, they heard my jaw drop. Baby bald eagles in Alaska turned to their parents and asked what that noise was.

I am forty-eight years old. For the first time in my life, it was being suggested *to my face* that I was closer to sixty than fifty. A whole new demographic opened up in front of me.

I realise I have greying, almost non-existent hair and a face that's been lived in by squatters, but did I look over fifty-five? Perhaps it was down to jet lag or the shock of fresh air ... something other than the truth? I was stunned. I must have looked like an angry Gordon Brown.

Gathering myself, I fixed Mr Happy with a stare and intoned, as calmly as I could: 'Are you suggesting that I'm over fifty-five? *Over* fifty-five?'

'Well, over-fifty-fives do benefit from a 10 per cent discount across the entire range, sir.'

'Brilliant. I'll be sixty next month, can you double-bag everything? My arthritic hands can't carry the way they used to. Plus if my back is any guide, there's a storm a-comin'.'

26 April–2 May

Be warned

This page contains jokes – from the start

You will find all sorts of ancient artefacts scattered through-out Broadcasting House. I'm going to resist the temptation to make a cheap joke at Corrie Corfield's expense here. I am in fact referring to pieces of kit: unassuming in themselves but part of our broadcasting heritage. Again, please cast Corrie from your mind. I shouldn't have mentioned her.

Near the back lifts, behind the glorious original reception area in BH, you'll find the actual microphone used by the old king to do one of his Christmas radio broadcasts. There is a photo of the king sitting at the mike, looking nothing at all like Colin Firth. Probably because it was a different king. A piece of broadcasting history, just sitting quietly under a protective case, while we modern-day broadcasters rush past wolfing our frothy cappuccinos and moist pastries.

In the corner of the café on the ground floor of New Broadcasting House sits something I could stare at all day. It's not a giant mirror, nor a large sign saying 'Do Not Blink at This Notice'. It is in fact a tiny piece of kit, in a protective clear casing, that used to beam into your living room.

To the untrained eye (mine) it looks from the side to be an old-fashioned camera, the kind you see in silent movies, where a man in tweed with a tripod holds aloft a giant flash that is so bright the people in the photograph are blinded.

Look from the front, though, and it is unmistakably a number 2. Do not insert any cheap joke here either. This little box was one of those that used to appear in vision on BBC2 while the continuity announcers intoned their stuff.

Just the number 2 made up of a series of lines that would – if you were lucky – separate to either side of the screen before joyously returning to re-create the number 2. Simpler times, the seventies.

The uncomplicated animation was, to my memory, a colourful, rather wondrous moment. Nowadays the visual feasts that appear between TV programmes are worthy of Academy Awards. Digital masterpieces created by people with the word 'creative' in their job titles, and which have core branding at their heart. Meanwhile, the sturdy workhorse that did years demonstrating that we weren't watching BBC1 sits motionless in the corner of a café, largely ignored. I don't think I've ever seen a sadder-looking number 2. And really you've got to stop that right now.

Modern continuity announcers have so much more to do than boom 'This is BBC1'. It might be my viewing habits, but every programme I watch now carries a lengthy warning beforehand. 'The following programme contains strong violence, scenes of a sexual nature, strong language and flashing images FROM THE START.' I love that final bit. Do people lunge for the remote to try to turn off the set before the filth-fest begins? And what's up with those programme-makers who filled their drama with sex, guns and potty-mouths, but not in the first minute? Not for them the coveted 'from the start' warning.

In fact, if the continuity warning doesn't include a 'from the start' I lunge for the remote to turn the thing off. If the well-heeled producers with their frothy cappuccinos and moist pastries can't organise something outrageous from the get-go, what are we paying the licence fee for? Come on BBC. Etc.

3–9 May

THE MOST BRILLIANT ARTICLE YOU'LL EVER READ

In an astonishing column for *Radio Times*, broadcasting legend Eddie Mair lifts the lid on the TRUTH behind writing columns, the HORRIFYING use of capital letters and the SHOCKING moment doctors revealed his head would explode if he ate one more tuna sandwich!

I'm exhausted just writing that; I wouldn't blame you if you needed a lie-down reading it. For both our sakes, I'll go at a more sedate pace for a moment. What's that? You're dying to read about my sandwich? Don't worry, we'll get to that.

Over the years, hardened newspaper readers have grown used to exciting headlines that don't seem to bear any relation to the words in the story. For example, you might read 'Fury Erupts Over . . .' in giant block capitals, only to find the story quotes someone saying, 'I'm a bit annoyed about . . .' The headline was something of a fib.

Then there are gossipy celebrity magazine covers so colourful that your eyes have to keep moving around the page to prevent them from bleeding. 'Susanna: My Alarm Clock Hell' is, it turns out, a searing five hundred words on how the new *Good Morning Britain* host once ran out of AAAs for her bedside timepiece.

The rest of the cover is devoted to lurid photos screaming of enormous weight loss/weight gain, and a photo of a sad-looking woman whose otherwise devoted husband is setting up a new life with their pet corgi. Oh, and there's always journalism's ultimate oxymoron, 'Jordan: Exclusive!'

By the way, the United Nations organisation set up to

preserve the world's punctuation (UNPUNCT!) estimates that these magazines are almost solely responsible for the planet's shockingly low reserves of exclamation marks. Dominic Lawson argues that's nonsense.

So we've learnt to take the headlines and hype with a pinch of salt. What gets on my nerves is how the habit has spread online and multiplied. Desperate for a click, websites promise 'the most brilliant wedding video you'll see'/'the most shocking ATM robbery in history'/'the cutest kitten playing with wool humanity will ever witness'.

Sure, for the first thousand times or so I fall for this kind of promotion. But each time the actual experience falls somewhat short of what was promised. A dull sense of disappointment momentarily sets in. Happily it can quickly be erased with this next link: 'the most hilarious laugh ever'. Seconds later, the disappointment returns, in a slightly darker shade of blue.

In a sense, you can't blame the sites. Clicks mean money. Where's the crime in a little overwriting? But I heard on Radio 4 the other day someone promising coverage of 'dramatic scenes in the courtroom'. Why not just let us hear what happened in the court and we can decide individually whether or not it was dramatic?

And now I feel doubly bad because you're patiently waiting for my tuna-sandwich story and on the strength of the article so far you're starting to doubt whether it's all I suggested at the start. You're right. There was this one time a doctor suggested that maybe I could lay off the tuna sandwiches. I don't think it was related to any medical condition; he'd just smelt my breath. Sorry, it's not much of a story.

But I promise, next week, the full and shocking truth about me, Fenella Fielding and a melon.

24–30 May

The big questions

Are suncream and after-sun the same?

One of the great things they say about being on holiday, as I was last week, is that it gives you time to think. Freed from the routines of everyday living, you suddenly have the space to think about humanity's great philosophical questions. Think about the ecological challenges the earth faces. Think about the cruelty of war, famine and disease.

Or in my case, think about whether suntan lotion and after-sun lotion are essentially the same thing. I mean, who would really know if canny manufacturers filled both products with identical white gloop?

I spent time in the supermarket staring at the respective lists of ingredients. Aqua seemed to be the main one. It's funny how plain old water becomes sophisticated aqua when the makers would like to divert attention from the fact you're mainly paying for stuff that falls from the sky.

The rest were very similar and seemed devoid of anything as natural as aqua. They put me in mind of chemistry lessons. I pondered wistfully that if I'd paid more attention at school, I might be able to fathom what was on these lists. As I daydreamt into the middle distance, the woman behind me in the checkout queue jabbed my ribs as if to say that I should really have done my ingredients-checking before coming to the till.

It's not just the great suntan lotion debate that transfixed me on holiday. There were other big questions I wrestled with as I lay in the sun, having slathered myself in after-sun.

Is 2-in-1 shampoo and conditioner really any different from

bog-standard shampoo? Would anything untoward happen to a woman who used men's shower gel? Why are drunken violent louts described in the newspapers as drunken violent louts – except when they are actors of a certain vintage, who are hailed as 'hell-raisers'? Why do the same newspapers spend 364 days a year viciously condemning hopelessly drunk people who go out and party late into the night, but on New Year's Eve the same people doing the same thing become 'revellers'?

Unsatisfyingly, I didn't come up with any decent answers to those questions. Worse, I began to question whether 'unsatisfyingly' is a legitimate word.

Tired of going round in circles in my mind, I picked up one of the books I'd packed for just this moment, when I wanted to lose myself in something, in the style of a Walnut Whip.

This, too, caused a quandary. It's a book I've been meaning to read for years ... one of those books people make a great fuss of. I prepared to open it for the first time. But I was torn. Read it, and know it? Or put it down and keep the anticipation for even longer? What a dilemma. I looked at the author's name on the cover and wondered, what would Joseph Heller do?

31 May–6 June

Merry Berry!

Don't laugh – Mary's inspired me to cook

I've just bought Mary Berry's new cookbook – the one that accompanies her recent TV series. In practically every photograph, whether she's handing out a slice of her salmon and asparagus terrine or slicing effortlessly through her flawless maple-glazed gammon with fresh apricot and ginger chutney, she looks to me to be the happiest person alive.

Take the photo of Mary as she guides us through the intricacies of her venison and chestnut pie. As Mary wields her trusty rolling pin she beams like a EuroMillions rollover winner. Preparing pastry has never made me anything other than grumpy, yet for Mary it looks to be the secret of eternal happiness.

Most of my forays into the kitchen involve pricking micro-wavable plastic, and those that don't – when I am inspired to follow a simple recipe – involve compound swearing. The only time I ever look as happy as Mary in the kitchen is when I've chucked another failed adventure in the bin and attacked the cooking sherry.

But here's the thing: Mary's smile inspires. It says to bumbling amateur cooks like me, 'Look, I'm having a ball doing this – you'll enjoy it too.'

Her happy confidence leaps off the page and makes me believe I can not only whip up one of her delicious treats, but thoroughly enjoy myself while I'm at it. I have plans to tackle one of her recipes this week. I will report back on whether it succeeds and whether I am hospitalised from laughing too much.

Right royal panic

One evening last week, in the middle of *PM*, my newsreading colleague turned to me when the microphones were off and said: '____ ____ is dead'. He used the name of a very senior member of the royal family.

We feared the dreaded time had come, and the BBC's

well-rehearsed plans for this sad moment would swing into action. It would fall to me to tell the nation of a very senior royal death, and then try to steer coverage for several hours. It's not a job I would relish.

Fifteen minutes later it transpired that the report had come from a fake Twitter account purporting to be that of a rival, well-respected news organisation. Checks were made, and the said royal was confirmed to be in fine fettle. The same cannot be said of my dry-cleaner, who is now declining all future business from me.

Narnia in Northampton

A friend has moved to Northampton and at the weekend I paid a visit. I'd been to Southampton, so why not collect the set? I arrived on Saturday evening and left Sunday morning so most of the shops were shut ... but what I saw made me want to plan a longer return visit.

Did you know Northampton has a fancy-dress store called Narnia Fancy Dress? How big do you think their back shop is?

And there are lots of independent tea and coffee places, including one called Are You Being Served? I fancy that Mrs Slocombe and Mr Humphries are in there, fawning over the customers, then bitching behind their backs.

And there's a mysterious venue called BBC. I put a photo of it on Twitter because I knew no one would believe me. Apparently BBC means 'Black Bottom Club: Members Only'. Fancy.

7–13 June

All hail!

How do weather presenters keep their cool?

For many listeners, the highlight of *PM* is just before the end of the programme when a person from the BBC Weather Centre appears, as if by magic, and, with little more than a crystal ball and some tarot cards, predicts what the weather will be like. I'm joking of course. They don't use tarot cards.

In times gone by, weather forecasters would have only a handful of outlets per day. They'd pop up on Radio 4 once in a while . . . do a bit at the end of the *Nine O'Clock News*, that late-night thing on BBC2 and that would be about it. These days, they do all of that but in addition have to service the BBC News channel, BBC World News, online, Twitter . . . they barely have time to look out the window to check if their forecasts were right.

Their appearance on *PM* is always the last act in a long and busy shift, and yet here's the thing they can all do: they sit down with only a satellite picture of the UK in front of them and talk, clearly, knowledgeably and to time, about the weather. It's often the most fluid and intelligible thing in the whole hour, and it's done without a script. Studio guests often marvel at this ability – gawping as the weather person weaves ninety seconds of perfect prose out of a map with some scribbles on it. I share their admiration. Understanding the weather, then having the ability to impart the information on radio, is an underrated skill. It's even more impressive when you consider the obstacles we sometimes place in the way of our weather staff.

The bit about talking 'to time' is especially impressive.

Despite our best efforts, the *PM* newshounds sometimes get our timings wrong. There can be many reasons for that. Lively discussions overrun their allotted time. Boring discussions overrun their allotted time. I won't shut up.

The effect on the poor meteorologist can be that they plonk themselves in the studio chair, ready to do their minute and a half of weather, only to be told by our studio director that they have only a minute. Or half a minute. Or, on one famous occasion that was entirely my fault, about fifteen seconds. They have almost no notice that their airtime has evaporated, yet somehow make it sound smooth and polished. They're sickeningly good broadcasters.

Merry Berry latest

And here's the urgent update I promised when I exclusively revealed my plan to emulate the great Mary Berry and knock up one of her famed salmon and asparagus terrines. Regrettably, I didn't visibly enjoy the process as much as Mary does. There was some frowning as I tussled with the clingfilm dispenser and I used a word I'm sure Mary has never uttered when I switched on the blender without its lid. The kitchen was such a disaster area that the UN sent aid.

But if I say so myself, the end product was a success. It looked the part and no one was hospitalised after eating it. (My definition of 'hospitalised' is an overnight stay.) I'll try more. In fact, my new cookbook, *Eddie Mair Scowls His Way through Mary Berry's Recipes*, will be on the shelves in time for Christmas. The ideal gift for an estranged ex, or a neighbour you're taking to court over the size of their hedge.

My masterpiece

The one interview I'll never forget

The thing I love about live broadcasting is this: blink and it's gone. If, like me, you're prone to saying the wrong thing, or saying nothing when you should have spoken, you can take comfort in the temporary nature of the live programme. Say it, and it's vanished; lost to the ether. As fleeting as a Cher retirement.

Wonder why the BBC insists that stuff on the iPlayer self-destructs after a week or a month? Secret deal with the NUJ to spare the blushes of goons like me.

People often come up to me in the street and they say: 'Eamonn, what's your favourite interview?' and are somewhat surprised to hear that I don't have one. Memorable interviewees? Sure – hundreds. But you know that feeling we all get after an argument when we think five minutes later of the really smart thing we should have said? That's every interview. Reflection only brings dismay that I said too much or too little or the wrong thing at the wrong time. That TV interview I did with Boris Johnson that caused such a fuss? I hated it. It was supposed to focus on our mutual love of salsa (dancing and sauce) but I allowed it to get sidetracked. I've never watched it back.

This cosy world where I'm never confronted with previous interviews has been shattered thanks to the work of the artist Bob and Roberta Smith. Don't be confused by the name: the artist is one man (and his real name is Patrick Brill).

Bob heard an interview we did on *PM* over Christmas last year with David Nott and decided to make it a work of art.

David is a surgeon but for the past twenty years or so, during his holiday time, he has gone to some of the world's trouble spots to use his surgical skills, working with Médecins Sans Frontières and the International Red Cross. Not for him the suntan oil and swim-up bar. David packed his bags and headed to every hell-hole we'd never want to visit. And a more modest, self-effacing person you would be hard pushed to find.

Our interview focused on his recent time in Syria. Over the course of twenty-five minutes David quietly and calmly described what he and his colleagues did every day, what he witnessed in Syria and how he dealt with it. He said things that shocked me. He said things that shocked me into silence. I was drained after the recording. After it was broadcast, many listeners told us they felt the same.

Bob heard the interview and decided to paint it. He went to the iPlayer, transcribed it, then painted the words in black on a white background – creating a permanent record. The finished article is nearly five metres high by four metres wide. Best of all, it's on display at the Royal Academy Summer Exhibition in London.

Bob kindly invited David and me for a preview. It was surreal for me, seeing an interview from the past thrust into the present in a strange form. I was forced to confront it. Seeing David's words in black and white got me emotional again. David was taken aback.

Because of Bob's work, David's words are haunting me anew. His ability to bring permanence to something usually so fleeting is making me reconsider the nature of what I do. Bob put it beautifully: 'The real reason I painted it was simple. I did not want it to fade.'

5–11 July

Radio gaga

Meet James, my youngest listener

I'm sorry, I haven't a clue about the recent row about *I'm Sorry I Haven't a Clue*. I only know what I've read about a handful of complaints alleging that Samantha's appearances on the programme are smutty (undeniable, I'd have thought) or sexist.

I'm told that, from time to time, the team have been asked to make the programme more accessible to new and younger listeners, who might wonder what they've stumbled across. The team's response is a good old-fashioned raspberry: they argue that listeners will find and understand the show in their own time and their own way, without having to explain every week what Mornington Crescent is about.

How to attract new listeners is the sort of thing radio executives wrestle with all the time; by which I mean they'll stare out their windows onto the Portland Place scene below, chewing on their pen tops, wondering how to get five-year-olds to listen to *Gardeners' Question Time*.

I gave a talk at a school recently, to an audience of fifteen-to seventeen-year-olds, and asked for a show of hands to indicate how many of them listened to the radio. Not a single hand went up, and it wasn't just because they'd all fallen asleep during my speech. Their media consumption is not that of their parents. It's all music-streaming services called Splat, file-sharing companies called Rhombus and chat services called Wheeeeeeeeeee. Will they find Radio 4 in twenty years' time? There is not an unchewed pen top in the whole of W1A.

At *PM* we've decided to woo the Wheeeeeeeeeee generation. I was inspired to do so when an email arrived from the BBC's Head of Digital Insertion. She urged me to pull my finger out and attached a YouTube video posted by the good people at Radio 2.

The video shows a toddler by the name of Daisy. Daisy is at home, surrounded by crayons and paper, as toddlers inevitably are. There is a radio on in the background: a news bulletin is just coming to an end – the newsreader says it's five past five. Next we hear the jingles signalling the start of Simon Mayo's fine show, and this sends young Daisy into ecstasy.

She becomes very animated, bouncing up and down with glee, repeatedly chanting 'Mayo'. The last time I saw a person that happy, his party had just done well in the European elections. Daisy loves her Simon, and she doesn't care who knows it.

Clearly, Radio 4 could not let this go unchallenged. I asked *PM* listeners if there were any toddlers out there who go into paroxysms of joy when I come on the air. I know. It was a big ask.

It seems the end of *PM* brings a lot of happiness (who'd have thought?) with the distinctive chimes of Big Ben providing more of a stimulus to young ears than the boring old pips at the beginning of the show. We've been sent videos showing that, across the nation, the bongs are a cue for the beginning of bathtime/bedtime/eat-time for many young children. Yet nowhere was there a Daisy-type.

I am indebted, however, to young James Mallory, and his mum Anne-Marie, in Inverness. They sent in a completely natural and unstaged photograph, showing that while James may be only fifteen weeks old, he's a dedicated *PM* listener. I salute you, James: what a discerning chap you are. I don't care if you're dribbling and incoherent – and you clearly don't mind listening to someone who is.

12–18 July

Max it up

These days, everyone's a critic

I recently spent some time with a gregarious travel writer – someone who's spent her professional life crisscrossing the globe so we don't have to. She was great company, until I made the mistake of asking her views on websites like TripAdvisor, where mere mortals can hold forth on the pros and cons of every aspect of travel.

Well, I haven't experienced a mood change like that since I asked Whoopi Goldberg whether the real reason that she wouldn't marry Peter Cushing was because she insisted on keeping her last name.

Let's just say the travel writer gave such websites no stars. Personally, I love the angry reviews. People fulminating about trouser presses that didn't work or an airline seat that didn't recline an extra half-centimetre. I like to imagine how angry they were at the time, given that hours later their online rage is such you'd think they'd just been placed in a trouser press.

It's not just travel sites. The other day I took a notion to a steak and kidney pie. Obviously I wasn't going to make one from scratch, so I toddled to an online supermarket to see what was new in the pie world. It turns out people will review pies too. Here are two actual reviews for exactly the same brand of pie:

1. 'For those who don't like kidney there are many steak pies on offer without it, but I like to find identifiable pieces of kidney in a steak & kidney pie and not have it hidden minced in the gravy.'

2. 'The kidney was a little too dominant in the mix and overshadowed an otherwise lovely pie. I would recommend leaving the kidney out and maxing up the steak content.'

Yes. Maxing up the steak content. I believe you'll find the same phrase in the teenage Egon Ronay's earliest attempts at food criticism.

Thinking of buying a bucket? Just a simple little bucket to do bucket-type things? Don't even consider such a significant purchase without first checking the bucket reviews. Again, here is something a real person took the trouble to contribute:

'This is such a useful little bucket. It is sturdy and well made for a thousand uses.'

I bought seven on the strength of that review. Maxed up the bucket content.

Mrs Lewis is raving about her sink strainer: '5 stars out of 5. I have had trouble with ill-fitting strainer plugs in my kitchen sink for years, but these are just the job! I know it might sound a bit odd raving about sink strainers, but they really have impressed me!'

Restaurant reviews are my favourite. Someone always has an experience so shocking, they would like the staff, manager and owner put to death by firing squad. Or, in this fine example from a steakhouse, by eating food from the kitchen: 'All steaks came out overdone. The very rude floor manager did change them but on several occasions advised us that they were cooked correctly. A medium steak is normally pink not grey in my experience. When we requested the bill and asked, because of the manager's rudeness, that the service charge be deducted he ranted again! Honestly, 1 out of 10 from our perspective.'

What you need after a meal like that is a good bucket. May I recommend . . .

2–8 August

Dear Reject . . .

How Newsnight *turned me down*

Hearty congratulations to Evan Davis, the man with Britain's most belligerent body clock. After years of going to bed in the middle of the afternoon to get up for work in the middle of the night, he has committed to getting up in the middle of the morning and not leaving the office until after midnight.

It's a great appointment by *Newsnight*, and even greater that it brings to an end the months of tedious speculation – and betting – about who could replace Mr Paxman. Speculation in which my name kept coming up. I realised how absurd it had all become when I was standing in the queue at William Hill's and the guy in front, Krishnan Guru-Murthy, turned round and asked whether I too was putting money on Andrew Neil.

For months, people have only asked me about three things.

1. Will you be going on *Newsnight*?
2. How do you keep your hair so vivacious?
3. Does Martha Kearney really keep all those bees or are they just special effects?

The answers, in no particular order, are:

1. It's a proprietary mint and jojoba rinse.
2. The bees are real, Martha is a CGI effect.
3. No, and they've made that quite clear in writing.

It was flattering to be linked to the post in the papers, but I do wish people hadn't put money on me. The reality is that *Newsnight* were pretty specific in their objections. Their letter was kind enough, but reading between the lines, I don't think they rated me. Let me quote it directly:

Dear Rejected Mair,

Thank you for your interest in *Newsnight* but regrettably you will not be considered for the post. Under the recently streamlined BBC Employment Guidelines, Chapter 456, Subsection 523, Paragraph 72, we are legally obliged to inform you why you would really suck at it. Here are some of the reasons:

1. We watched video recordings of your previous appearances. Enough said. But if you would like further guidance . . .

2. Your on-screen manner resembles someone who's having an AK47 pointed at him by the camera operator.

3. You have a face for radio.

4. And a body.

5. The feature for which you were responsible on Radio 4's *Broadcasting House*, known as 'The Donald Rumsfeld Soundbite of the Week'.

6. Every time you presented *Newsnight*, you were either apologising for something, or did something you should have been apologising for. We think it's time to move on from that.

7. We have viewed the 'Best of Eddie' tape the *Newsnight* producers put together for you after your final appearance on the programme. It consisted entirely of awkward silences.

8. Is that suit drip-dry?

9. Elaine Stritch would do a better job than you. Even in her current condition.

10. See number 2.

Best wishes, HR

30 August–5 September

Praise be to Paxo

His one-man show is a triumph (honest)

Jeremy Paxman is holding a sign pointing to a Golf Sale, and looking forlorn. Now I come to think of it – do those signs ever actually point to genuine golf sales? There seem to be so many of them. Are Britain's side streets really jam-packed full of bargain tartan trousers and competitively priced spherical Dunlops?

Or is it all a giant con perpetrated on hapless middle-aged men in bright sweaters who innocently follow the sign-holders' directions only to be mugged in a dimly lit alley by a gang of twelve-year-olds?

Jeremy Paxman wielding a Golf Sale sign would appear to indicate he has fallen on hard times, post-*Newsnight*. Don't worry, it's all part of his act. Literally.

I saw him holding the sign ten days ago, at a London-based preview of the one-man show he went on to take to the Edinburgh Fringe. My presence at the preview was, in itself, remarkable. I never get invited anywhere by people who know me, because they know me. I never go anywhere when I'm invited by strangers, because you should never talk to strangers. This invitation came from the woman who connects me to Jeremy, my wonderful agent, Bebe Glazer.

(That's not her real name but I have always referred to her that way. *Radio Times* libel lawyers have asked me not to detail the reasons for that. Let me put it like this: devotees of Dr Frasier Crane will recall his agent, a Ms Bebe Glazer, a rather ferocious woman with a mad glint in her eye who would have you checking for your wristwatch after a long hug. 'Lady Macbeth without the sincerity,' as Niles once put it.)

Anyhoo, my wonderful agent invited me along to see *Paxo* and I told her it was an offer I couldn't refuse. She released my arm from its twisted position behind my back and slammed a pair of free tickets into my quivering palm.

You might assume I would feel obliged, in the circumstances, to give Jeremy's show a positive review, given our professional connection, the freebie tickets and the whispered threat from Bebe that if I wrote a bad word about the show she would book me as a guest speaker on the planned seven-week long pleasure cruise around the Alaskan coast: 'Robert Peston Explains Economics In Five Different Languages (None Of Them English)'.

It was a full house. Jack Whitehall was in the audience, as was former BBC director-general George Entwistle. And me.

I had been tipped off that there would be a chance for audience members to ask questions of Mr P, but I had also been warned by Bebe not to ask – and I quote – 'any of your stupid smartarse nonsense'. As a reminder, the 9mm silencer of a Beretta 92FS was nestled snugly in the small of my back, where I also keep a lot of fat deposits. That gun was lodged there so long I can almost feel it now, as I write this column.

I have explained to my agent (who is *not* here right now), that the column will be published after Jeremy's Edinburgh run is over, but nonetheless she has politely asked that I write a few words entirely of my own volition with my good arm, featuring my true opinions about the evening. Here goes: 'Jeremy Paxman's one-man show *Paxo* is brilliant in every respect. Laugh? My pants will never dry. Magnificent. His agent deserves some kind of award.'

13–19 September

Fruit loops

Only fools mess with mangoes

Marks & Spencer get a lot of bad press. If it's not their pants, it's their new returns policy that some people consider to be pants. But never mind all that. I saw something in a store the other day that made me pant.

I was in the mood for mango (they can't touch you for it) and began eyeing the chilled shelves of the food department. I didn't want the tiresome mango that involves taking a week off work to wield a serrated-edged knife, faff with the skin, find the stone, make it look like a hedgehog, and then have a lie-down, exhausted.

I quite fancied an environmentally disastrous but oh-so-delicious mango that someone had already prepared, and chopped up into bite-size pieces, stored hygienically in a little plastic pot.

Nestling on the shelf, there it was: a simple little tub

of mango. I reached for the unassuming portion of fruity delight when something about the product startled me. No, it wasn't a dead mouse or a human ear. Nor had the mango pieces mysteriously gathered themselves to represent the image of Jesus Christ or Diana Beard from *The Great British Bake Off*.

What startled me was the description of the product printed on the thin plastic film covering the goodies. You might have expected 'Mango', 'Diced Mango', or maybe 'Chopped Mango in its Own Delicious Juices'. They would have been excellent suggestions.

No. Marks & Spencer chose to describe its chopped mango thus: 'Mango Madness'. Yes, my jaw fell to the floor too. No mean feat with these chins.

I stared at the label. It did indeed say 'Mango Madness'. I lifted up the tub to inspect its contents from beneath. It was just mango. Chopped-up bits of mango. I looked at the label again. It still said 'Mango Madness'.

Clearly somewhere in M&S head office there had been a big meeting (with great sandwiches) called by the Head of Fruit in Plastic Tubs. 'I've become increasingly concerned that some of our fruit tubs are not punching above their weight, and I'd like to brainstorm exciting new names for flogging the same old stuff. Let's go round the table, starting with you, Tarquin.'

'Um, Delicious Mango?'

'What about *The Great British Bake Off* Mango? That's a very hot brand now ... '

'Last Mango in Paris?'

'Mango Fandango?'

'Mango Leadbetter?'

'What about Sectioned under the Mental Health Act Mango?' suggests an up-and-coming executive who started out in ladies' underwear, but is now very big in men's made-to-measure.

The Head of Fruit in Plastic Tubs fixes the spotty youth with a stare. 'You might be on to something there, you know. It's perhaps a little elaborate. Could we workshop it quickly?'

There is a quick-fire exchange of ideas with everyone shouting excitedly: 'Crazy Mango!', 'Certifiable Mango!', 'One Flew Over the Mango!', 'Broadmango!'

Then, with the sort of flourish that made her the youngest Head of Fruit in Plastic Tubs since 1893, the boss declared: 'I've got it! We'll call the chopped-up mango Mango Madness!'

They cheered, and no one considered that the real madness was not in the tub at all.

20–26 September

The real Joan

I hear the sadness behind the jokes

Friday night at the Royal Festival Hall in London and I'm watching Anthony Dominick Benedetto saunter round the stage. I confess I'm slightly troubled. This is not Mr Benedetto's fault. Tony Bennett's stage presence is a transcendent thing of wonder to me. It's not only the singing. To say Tony Bennett just sings is to say Rolex just makes watches.

I've never seen a man look more comfortable in a suit. Perhaps he sleeps in one. I bet when he wakes in the morning there is not a crease in it.

What's he doing on the stage? Prowling is not the right word – that suggests menace. Does he own the stage? No, he's renting it from the Royal Festival Hall. I would say he is relaxing all over the stage. He is performing to a vast room with only a four-piece band for cover, yet he could be meandering round Lidl, pleased as punch at the bargains. I always try to see Tony Bennett whenever he comes to the UK. He is a joy.

Yet I'm troubled.

Joan Alexandra Molinsky is on my mind. I always try to see Joan Rivers whenever she comes to the UK. I was there at the Leicester Square Theatre in 2008 when she gave us her 'Work in Progress'. Four years later, I was there one Saturday night for the Brighton leg of the tour she'd entitled, with great foresight, 'Now or Never'.

In October 2013 I booked tickets for the October 2014 Joan Rivers show in Brighton. I was slightly annoyed with Joan for apparently being unaware of my work commitments. She scheduled the start of her Friday-night show at 7.30 p.m. It would be impossible to reach the Brighton Centre after the end of *PM* at six o'clock, even if I borrowed Rona Fairhead's chopper. So I booked the day off work. But then, as if to further annoy me, Joan died. She was eighty-one: seven years younger than Mr Bennett, though in fairness he seems to have aged more.

I have friends who went to see Kate Bush perform live recently and their paroxysms of delight were a vicarious thrill. How nice to have public figures who can do that for you. I have so few heroes. Tony. Joan. Rona, of course. The older we get, the more funerals we go to. The fewer concerts.

Tony Bennett lifted me from a melancholic mood. I'd arrived at the Festival Hall fresh from the first *PM* after the death of Joan Rivers. We re-broadcast part of her revealing interview with Dr Pamela Stephenson Connolly for More4 in 2008. Joan discussed her husband's suicide, her bulimia and her desire for financial security. The desire, no doubt, that kept her touring. Read this extract and tell me it doesn't make you feel sad too:

Pamela Connolly: What do you see about your body weight when you look in the mirror?

Joan Rivers: Fat. Fat, fat, fat.

PC: Joan, you're not fat. I'm wondering about body dysmorphic disorder, where a person has an inaccurate view of their own body.

JR: No man ever told me I had a good body. And trust me, I was listening for that. No man ever told me I was beautiful.

PC: What nice things did they say to you?

JR: You're wonderful, you're terrific . . . I've had great relationships but no man's ever said any big compliment about my body, ever.

4–10 October

I'm going gaga

This week I lost the plot – and my wallet

There was a film I wanted to see at the cinema last week. I already knew a bit about it. The early reviews had been generally positive. This being 2014, I booked a ticket online, printed it off at home, then wafted to the cinema in good time for the scheduled start of the forty-six adverts, one thousand and seven trailers and four million idents before the actual film, alerting me to all the production companies and distributors involved in making it.

This being London, popping to the cinema involved a walk, two Tube journeys and a hitchhike, but I was in such good spirits about the prospect of the film the trip left me unmangled.

Sashaying into the foyer, I fixed the ticket woman with my most winning smile. (Try to recall the leer of Sir Anthony Hopkins in his best-ever role. No, it's not *84 Charing Cross Road*. It's not *Dracula* either, though I see where you're going with that. Look, it doesn't matter – forget I mentioned him.)

I fixed the ticket woman with a dazzling smile and proffered my carefully printed tickets. She looked at me as though I'd just whacked her over the head with a BAFTA. 'This is for *next* Saturday,' she said.

I wanted to lunge at her like some cannibalistic serial killer. 'What?' I asked, suddenly crestfallen like Emma Thompson in *The Remains of the Day*. The woman pointed at the date on the piece of paper. She was right. I had meticulously paid for, downloaded and printed tickets for the following week.

Mortified, I turned on my heels (well, they went with my dress) and marched out of the cinema, hoping the same woman would not be in the foyer next week when I turned up with my dog-eared ticket. Luckily, by the time I had made the return journey home by Tube, bus, hitchhike and camel, it was almost time to leave the house again for the cinema.

I try to learn lessons from life's rich experiences. For example, I know now never to accept an arm-wrestling bet from Fi Glover, or to believe Martha Kearney when she promises 'Honestly, they won't sting'. My self-inflicted ticketing wound reminded me to tend to details more carefully. It also taught me that if I'm doing this kind of thing at the age of forty-eight, I'm likely to be gaga before I'm sixty.

Two days later, I was having a panic when I lost my wallet. You'll be familiar with the feeling, I'm sure. Your wallet or purse is not in its usual place at home, so you check pockets, bags and drawers. I was perfectly calm. I was sure it had to be at home somewhere.

A full twenty minutes later, I was no longer sure of anything. I'd checked all the usual places three times each. All the unusual places twice. I even checked it wasn't in the bathroom, for goodness' sake. Before long I was fumbling down the back of chairs I hadn't sat in, checking trousers I hadn't worn and fumbling in that drawer with the broken tools, dead batteries and Deutschmarks. There was no sign of my wallet.

I was just about to phone all the credit card companies to alert them to the disaster, pausing only to wonder how I could do so when their phone numbers were on the backs of my missing credit cards. By this time I was sweating like Bogie in *Key Largo*. I headed to the kitchen to get some cooling ice-cold water from the fridge.

My wallet was on the second shelf.

18–24 October

RIP *Dallas*

I'll never forget the night I met JR

And now a flashback to one of the proudest moments of my life. As ever, you can insert your own flashback/harp noise/ screen dissolve here, for added authenticity: Larry Hagman has just bumped fists with me. I'm introduced as being from the BBC.

Larry 'Oh, they used to broadcast our show.'

Me 'I know. I'm here to tempt you back.'

Larry 'How much money do you have on you?'

Harp effect/screen dissolve. It is the present day once again and you are reading this column, perhaps wondering why.

That flashback was from the Channel 5 launch party for the *Dallas* reboot. Re-cowboy-boot, if you will. I was in the room as JR, Bobby and Sue Ellen (who appeared to be on the sauce again) pretended to be actors for the night, promoting the return of the TV show that has for years epitomised eighties flashback TV shows. Newer cast members were there too, including the gardener from *Desperate Housewives*, but those of us of a certain vintage (shut it, missus) had eyes only for the oil barons who might have seen bigger balls in their lifetimes, but were kind enough to treat the Channel 5 shindig with the reverence of a Southfork poolside wedding.

Three seasons later, having revelled in the return of *Dallas*, and having survived, with the tormented scriptwriters, the death of Larry Hagman, I stuck with the show even after Channel 5 shunted it to midnight.

I won't lie to you. Of late I had very little understanding of who was double-crossing whom. I blame myself for that, rather than the writers. For example, in the excellent but bloody *Sons of Anarchy*, I'm never certain which murderous gang has quintuple-crossed which loathsome bunch of killers until the shoot-out.

The brooding glances and arched eyebrows might be enough of a signal to most viewers of a character's disgust or an impending showdown, but until actors are being zipped up in body bags I'm more confused than Sue Ellen spied through the bottom of a glass.

All of which brings me to the news you might have heard: that after three seasons, the re-versioned *Dallas* has gone the same way as Jock, Digger and both Miss Ellies. Falling viewing figures in the US meant that a fourth season was as likely as a live appearance from Mr Hagman.

It's a shame. The new version had fizz, verve and energy. But then so does a can of Red Bull. The writers honoured the *Dallas* tradition, the actors gave it the appropriate amount of welly, and much of the whole sparkling pile of nonsense was beautifully shot in Dallas itself, the way JR used to be. They made the city look more gorgeous than it is.

Dallas will live on in my heart. Whenever I see a man in a Stetson, a woman with quivering lips or someone being pushed sideways into a kidney-shaped pool, I will think of it. There is a chance that, like so many of its cast members, it will return from the dead.

And I'll always have the memory of meeting the star of the show, Larry Hagman. A man who survived contract battles with CBS, problems with alcohol and a liver transplant, only to die three months after bumping fists with me.

25–31 October

Nice work

My life as a travel journalist

I am not a travel journalist. Let's be candid, the jury's out on whether I'm any kind of journalist, but travel journalist I am not. So brace yourselves, as this week's column is devoted to my first-ever trip to Nice (it's in the south of France, you know) this past weekend.

Simon Calder, senior travel editor at the *Independent*: now *there's* a travel journalist. He's famous around the world. In Spain they call him Señor Travel Editor.

PM is one of the many programmes prone to phoning Simon because he knows literally everything there is to know about travel. The address of the best awning to stand under in Hong Kong to protect you from a sudden rain storm? Simon will know. How to transport golf clubs and a wedding cake down the Amazon without either getting wet? Simon will know.

Cost of a three-star hotel room in Berlin, not too far from an underground station but where the second-floor rooms get enough dappled sunlight in the late afternoon so as to wake you from a successfully executed nap thanks to the hotel's strict 'no babies crying in the afternoon during Oktoberfest' rule? Simon will know.

But that's not me. I learnt I wasn't a travel journalist when they hired me to present a travel programme for Radio 4. It was the early nineties: *Breakaway* on a Saturday morning. Do you remember it? It had that jaunty theme tune that vividly recalled the twenties, as did the pay. You're most likely to recall the glory *Breakaway* years when Bernard Falk did a fine job hosting, or perhaps the insanely knowledge-able contributions of Nigel Coombs from the *Travel Trade Gazette*.

Mercifully, the production staff were talented. Like all the best producers, they did their best to paper over cracks in the presenter's abilities. In my case it was more than cracks. Are you familiar with the Grand Canyon? It's in America, I think.

My first trip was to Le Touquet, in France. A proper travel journalist would have dug into the soul of the place and painted vivid word pictures. I remember walking the length of the beach, spouting irrelevant nonsense into the tape recorder while the exasperated producer *just* kept a lid on his temper by gently suggesting we take the best of takes two, five and sixty, and go for *just* one more. How he didn't punch me I don't know. I might even have described the place as 'nice'.

Oh! That reminds me I'm supposed to be telling you about Nice! It's not just a biscuit you know! Ha-ha-ha-ha. Come to think of it, neither was *Breakaway*. I don't recall too many trips after Le Touquet. We went to French-speaking Canada (which I probably described as *agréable*) and I remember an ill-fated live outside broadcast from Bath, where we lost all communication with London just before transmission. I still can't think of the Pump Room without feeling a certain tightening.

The closest I got to being a proper travel journalist during my time on *Breakaway* was on a big media trip somewhere. On to our bus stepped Judith Chalmers, the woman who personified travel. I think I heard angels sing. I was too starstruck to introduce myself (my constitution was recalling the Pump Room) but there she was, proving that although I wasn't a travel journalist, at least I was moving in the right circles.

I realise I've forgotten to write about Nice. Next week, I promise.

1–7 November

To see you Nice

My elegant sojourn on the French Riviera

Now that British Summer Time has gone the same way as *Dallas*, Spangles and my hair, I thought you might appreciate a trip down memory lane with me to sunnier times. I promised you last week a proper review of my trip to Nice and I'm a man of my word, or my name isn't Arthur Mullard.

I arrived for a cheeky long weekend in a place I'd never been. I wasn't sure how to dress but was inspired before departure by re-watching Hitchcock's *To Catch a Thief*, with Cary Grant and Grace Kelly. It's set in Nice and its environs (see how I slip so easily into the local tongue), so I reckoned if my wardrobe echoed that of a Hollywood style icon, I wouldn't go far wrong.

On reflection, while the halterneck beach top and Capri pants were a triumph in daytime, the blue chiffon gown was a touch too formal for the casual dining experience offered by the Promenade des Anglais McDonald's. Later, I told my dry cleaner that the ketchup stains were blood droplets but his eyes betrayed disbelief.

I found Nice charming. Anywhere that has a shop dedicated to fresh macaroons must be on to something. And they've got that promenade malarkey down to a T. Oodles of space for pedestrians to meander, separated from whizzing cars by a big double bike lane. Having gone to all that trouble, though, I wondered why they dumped a million pebbles on the beach rather than soft-on-the-soles sand. I searched the promenade end to end for a flip-flop shop but to no avail.

The five-star hotel was too classy for me, although I always feel that way about hotels regardless of the number of stars they have. The opulent surroundings did afford me the chance to see close up some spectacular foyer floral displays, and boutiques offering jewels so expensive I'm not surprised Hitchcock found the place riddled with cat burglars. Thankfully, the only robbery was in the hotel bar where they wanted nine euros for 250ml of beer.

I walked into the hotel one afternoon behind an exquisitely dressed French couple – in their sixties or seventies, perhaps.

They could have been Grace and Cary in their later years, effortlessly oozing style and elegance. I prayed they didn't turn round to see me, shambling through reception like a tramp at a wedding reception.

I couldn't take my eyes off her and only when I watched them disappear into the lift did I realise what was so mesmerising. She was gliding. She glided. (She glid?) Was it class? Great deportment? Was she somehow on castors? No, I could see her putting one leg in front of the other yet she could have been floating on air. I saw them the next morning emerging from the breakfast room, radiating serenity. She was still gliding, like a beautiful Dalek.

But, look, you didn't come here for wistful nonsense like that. I may not be a travel journalist but I can pass on one genuinely useful hard-nosed tip for Nice. There's a big hill at one end of the prom, with what appears to be a thousand beautiful steps to the waterfall-festooned summit. If you're a Kenyan athlete, do have a jog to the top. For the rest of us, please take the time to locate the not-at-all-well-signposted lift those sneaky French people have hidden away inside the rock. Take the lift, and avoid the heart attack.

You're welcome.

8–14 November

Theatre of dreams

If you like Radio 4, you'll love this . . .

I was surrounded by Radio 4 listeners. It was not the usual nightmare in which they are screaming obscenities, trying to beat me to death with back copies of *Radio Times*. This was reality. Everywhere I looked, there were women and men of a certain age, sporting perfectly coiffured grey hair or a bald patch. And in my case, both.

It was the Saturday matinée of a new stage production entitled *But First This* – billed as 'A Musical Homage to Radio 4' at a theatre some distance from London's glittering West End. You've heard of 'Off Broadway' and 'Off Off Broadway'. This production required me to travel so far west I passed gold prospectors en route.

I travelled up hill and down dale to get there (well, along the M4, certainly), all to see a theatre production about the place from which I generally try to escape on a Saturday afternoon.

The venue was a small but beautifully crafted theatre called the Watermill. It's in the picturesque village of Bagnor in west Berkshire. The theatre gets its name from the working watermill churning away at the core of the building. Hats off to the person who decided what that watermill needed was a theatre built around it.

Sometimes people ask me what Radio 4 newsreaders do when they're not intoning world events or artfully guiding the network from a trailer about piles into a teaser for *The Bottom Line*. Well, it varies. Corrie Corfield, for example, works part-time at the circus. I'm not allowed to reveal her precise role, but let's just say she doesn't shave. Vaughan Savidge tends to his priceless collection of porcelain Robin Cook figurines. And Susan Rae is forever trying to finish her first novel. Boy, is she a slow reader.

What about Kathy Clugston? Sure, she can dazzle listeners with that unmistakable Celtic lilt (she's Welsh, I think) and if you have a certain kind of satnav Kathy will confidently guide you over a cliff of your choice.

For the past few years, whenever Kathy has come in to read

the news on *PM* I've noticed a certain frown upon her usually sunny countenance. I am nothing if not super-perceptive, so out of the blue one day I said to her, 'Kathy, you have the look of someone who, about ten years ago, had the dream of a stage show about Radio 4 that is now close to fruition in a theatre with some kind of water contraption in it. A show in which you do the book, lyrics and the music, and additional lyrics are by Desmond O'Connor.'

Well, OK, so I lifted some of that from the competitively priced programme that I clutched expectantly as the show began. I was a little nervous. What if it was rubbish? Could I tell Kathy that to her face? Of course not. I would just write something scathing in *Radio Times*.

In any case, I didn't feel obliged to Kathy. After all I'd had to *pay for my own ticket*. But I will get over that. Eventually.

In truth, *But First This* is quite brilliant. If you like Radio 4, you'll love it. Witty and knowing, satirical and even sentimental. It's a rollicking production bursting with energy and ideas. And the cast works harder than anyone at Radio 4. Sorry to gush, but my only criticism is that I wasn't mentioned more often. Oh, and the lack of a free ticket. It runs only until 8 November, but perhaps later at a theatre near you? I hope so.

15–21 November

My *One Show* diary

Here's what Alex Jones is really like . . .

Some weeks ago I promised you the inside story of *The One Show* and I am a man of my word. Especially if that word is 'liar'. Several people were startled by my unexpected appearance in their living rooms one Monday night recently but it was all hushed up and they agreed not to press charges.

Even more people were startled by my unexpected appearance in their living rooms one Monday night recently on their televisions. There I was, sitting next to Alex Jones while Matt Baker had a holiday, presumably in the countryside.

I was carefully selected as Matt's stand-in because BBC bosses are suddenly anxious to get older faces on screen. Luckily for me, I look older than the original Captain Birdseye, without the beard but with the unmistakable whiff of fish.

Only occasionally did the youthful production team call me Grandpa, and they thoughtfully left some incontinence pads for me in Matt's dressing room, where I squatted for four days (unrelated medical issue).

The One Show occupies a bright airy office on the seventh floor of the Peel Wing of Broadcasting House, next door to the Anna Wing Wing. There's a great view over Mary Poppins-style London rooftops and of the BT Tower. Contrast this with the accommodation *PM* enjoys four floors below. Virtually no natural light and a ceiling so low Sandi Toksvig can't stop stooping when she stops by.

What's Alex Jones like, you ask? Well, she kindly held my hand (figuratively) throughout the week and held my hand (literally) on one occasion when I broke down in helpless tears at first sight of all the natural daylight in the office.

I've had the displeasure of working with co-presenters who gleam and grin for the cameras but are dead behind the eyes when the red light goes off. Alex, by contrast, was fun to be around all the time – a very generous co-host. And I don't just mean the twenty-pound notes I swiped from her purse.

Here then are exclusive extracts from the *One Show* diary I pretended to keep.

MONDAY Elijah Wood: chatty and cheery on-air and off, despite flying in from the US only that morning. He did say his arms were tired.

TUESDAY Steve Backshall from *Strictly* joined us on the only sofa visible from space. One thing led to another and by the end of the show, several viewers had sent in photos of their hairy chests. Mainly men.

WEDNESDAY An hour-long show that began with Alex and me being hauled into vision in a vintage car. Some concern in rehearsal that the old banger wouldn't get going on cue but I managed. Griff Rhys Jones was our guest and when we shook hands before the show he said he'd heard me on *PM* and seen me do *Newsnight*.

He shook my hand for a long time, staring, looking me up and down, only to inform me I was too tall. Panic stations midway through the show when I lost all contact with the production gallery. Furtive checking by the sound man revealed everything was in place. In desperation, with seconds to go before I was in vision, he took a pin to the inside of my earpiece. Miracle! I could hear again! Diagnosis: waxy build-up.

THURSDAY Grayson Perry: liked him very.

22–28 November

Demon barber

How my haircut turned into torture

I had a horrific experience at the barber's yesterday. No, it wasn't the bit where he holds up the mirror to reveal my bald spot. I'm used to that now.

My bald spot is the polar opposite of the polar ice caps. Those graphics on the TV news that show the ice shrinking? Run them in reverse to understand the remorseless advance of my hairlessness. Nigel Lawson walked past me during a haircut once and said, 'Even I can't dispute that's happening.'

I like my barber's. There's never much of a queue, there's always a radio station playing today's best music variety and, judging by the photos festooning the walls, they've had a lot of famous people in.

The barbers themselves aren't chatty. This is a blessing. They seem to hail from a part of the Middle East where spoken English is as broken as the peace process, and they have the same trouble understanding me. Thankfully, I have so little hair and such simple needs my desires can be success-fully communicated through hand signals and smiles. There was only one occasion when my rudimentary semaphore let me down, but in the barber's defence, bubble perms were in at the time, and it did wash out within a week.

What happened yesterday, you ask? I know in this column I am prone to flights of fancy, whimsy and even elaborate fiction, but I swear to you everything you're about to read is true.

We were coming to the end of the haircut – I hadn't detained him long – when the barber began pointing

manically at my ears. I was about to take issue with his rudeness when it dawned on me he wanted to trim the tiny white
hairs there. I'd had such a procedure before, so I nodded my
approval and settled back to enjoy the aural buzz.

'Treading,' he said. I gave him a quizzical look.
'TREADING!' he shouted. I still had no idea what he was
blithering on about, but he seemed enthused, so who was I to
spoil his fun? I smiled, sat back, closed my eyes and relaxed.

When nothing happened, I opened one eye to see what
was occurring. The barber, a man to whom I have done no
harm, and have been known to tip, was frantically unreeling
a long piece of thread. I closed my eye again and began to
wonder what he would want with thread, and how did it
relate to my hairy lobes?

Seconds later, I understood. He was using a twisted thread
to yank stray hair off my ears. I literally jumped. He was
smiling down at me. 'Treading!' he beamed. 'Sore for while,
but good!'

I felt a tear forming, as he went about my fizzog. My ears,
forehead and cheeks all came under attack. I resisted my
natural instinct – to yell 'That hurts!' and run screaming
from the shop – and imagined this was what grown men and
women did all the time. I have friends who wax, and know
women who have given birth. Was this the pain they were
talking about?

After five minutes of my unexpected white-knuckle ride, it
stopped. Suddenly a huge hot towel splatted my countenance
and mummified me. Everything stung.

And then his face appeared. Grinning, thumbs held up triumphantly. I smiled and walked with all the dignity I could
muster to the till.

No tip.

29 November–5 December

Up, up and away

I'm almost fifty – time to do something new

I am now in my fiftieth year. Thankfully *Radio Times* is still using a completely up-to-date photo of me, so readers are spared the full horror, but reaching my forty-ninth birthday this month has suddenly got me thinking about what November 2015 will have in store, should I survive until then.

Does Saga write to you automatically? Will I start getting junk mail from the makers of reclining armchairs with adjustable footrests? Is it really time to consider a cruise? How close *is* the nearest loo?

On this page over the years I have carefully charted my decline into (further) decrepitude and I am confident that by the time I'm fifty I will have made further shuffling steps in that direction. My already failing eyesight suggests milk-bottle bifocals will be all the rage on my face before long. An ear trumpet will become my best friend. My remaining hair will fall out. And that nagging sense that there's something I've forgotten will be ... that French phrase in italics that suggests something really commonplace. It'll come to me when I've stopped thinking about it.

Talking of hair, I recounted recently a brief session in the barber's chair that turned into a *Sweeney Todd*-style marathon. My stylist embarked on a mission to remove the unwanted hairs from my countenance by doing something called threading: using thread to yank said hairs from my face. It was as painful as it sounds; the only upside to the lack of warning being that I didn't have time to anticipate the pain.

And so it was the weekend before my birthday – Remembrance Sunday – when friends insisted we should meet in London for a nice celebratory lunch. At least I think that's what they said. Why do people mumble so much these days?

I arrived at the agreed meeting place in Vauxhall but instead of being whisked off somewhere swanky we caught the 344 bus.

The route took us past many lovely sights: Battersea Power Station, the dog and cat home, the site of the new American embassy, and best of all a shop called Door World. Or House of Doors. Or something. But it was a shop that specialised in doors. Isn't that great? Ten years ago I'd have called that a pointless waste of real estate but, heading for my fifties, I cannot wait to go!

It became clear I would not be going to lunch when I was marched off the bus to a helipad. Yes, I had been given the birthday gift of my first-ever helicopter flight. I am scared of heights.

My friends correctly anticipated that advance warning would have sent me into a frenzy of worry about helicopter safety. Instead, within minutes of realising what was happening I was safely strapped into the back of a shiny helicopter, headphones on, about to swirl above the streets of London, making everyone look up and complain about the racket of the damn chopper.

With no time to fret, I was up and away and suddenly realising what Noel Edmonds has been on about all these years. Helicopters are fun! Down below, the Shard looked more transparent than from ground level, we peeped inside the Palace of Westminster, and the poppies and people at the Tower of London could be seen to their best advantage.

Why had I been afraid of this all these years? It was

exhilarating, and less painful than threading. Maybe my fifties won't be so bad.

Ooh, *de rigueur*.

6–12 December

Going ... gong

Memories of the radio award are, er, hazy

I am pleased to announce that *PM* is the Best News and Current Affairs radio programme of all time. That is my slightly over-generous interpretation of the news that this year's Radio Academy Awards were the last, at least in their present form. Since there will not be any more, and since *PM* won in that category this year, I claim the prize for the programme in perpetuity. Sue me.

The awards were undoubtedly the most sought-after awards in what is described as the radio industry. No one ever actually calls it that, except in sentences referring to the Radio Academy Awards. (It's not much of an academy either. Everyone who attends gets expelled in the end for talking too much in class.)

The demise of the awards, after more than thirty years, has left me faintly nostalgic – in the way that a burp can make you nostalgic for your most recent meal. My memories of the ceremonies are slightly hazy: the passage of time has not improved my powers of recall, not helped by the possibility that there may have been occasions when, to calm my nerves, I had a small sherry during the awards.

I attended my first in 1994 – I think they were held at lunchtimes in those days – and was never more dazzled by the occasion than then. Our programme won, so that was exciting. We were presented with the award by Moira Stuart, so I was already very happy, and then Kenny Everett took to the stage to win an outstanding contribution award. A little frail, very funny, and THERE in the flesh. Unforgettable. Not long after, his spectacular lifetime was cut short, and his contribution to radio silenced. I wonder how he would be using his talents today.

On another occasion, again having tried exuberantly to steady my nerves, I playfully made a remark to a senior industry person about two of her physical attributes. Recalling the remark at 4 a.m., I woke in a cold sweat. She graciously accepted my email of apology. I am an idiot.

A lot of nerves needed to be calmed at the awards ceremony every year. The event lasted at least four hours, and as time passed the acceptance speeches would become more vituperative, slurred and peppered with words that would have Ofcom spluttering into its cocoa. By the final hour, most of the people in the ballroom of London's Grosvenor House Hotel had long since stopped listening to the ceremony, and were engrossed in hearty sessions of champagne-buying and back-slapping (if they'd won) or recrimination and declarations of how pointless the bloody awards were (if they'd lost).

Radio people loved to win the awards and loved to complain about the ceremony. I certainly whined about it, but now that it's no more I'm sheepishly sentimental. Besides anything else it was a great place to meet old friends, and occasionally see radio heroes. I'd get to see Peter Allen once a year, slap Nick Ferrari on the back, and get a slap in the face from Corrie Corfield for no apparent reason.

For a few thrilling hours we, the unseen people who made radio happen, got their moment in the sun – or at least under some chandeliers, before emerging, unrecognised, into Park Lane, and another year of obscurity.

Nightmair

I had a terrible dream the other night that I was alone in a room with Donald Trump.

13–19 December

Done driving

I won't miss those wide boys at the garage

I have given up car ownership. I did it to help the environment, ease our congested roads and support our public transport system. Please send your champagne and other congratulatory gifts to me at *RT*. I thank you in advance.

No, don't. Those laudable motives did not drive me to stop driving. I just stopped driving.

PM's former home at BBC Television Centre was far easier for me to reach by car than Tube. But Broadcasting House is eminently Tube-able. After we moved back there, the final months of my car's lease saw it sitting outside the house acting as a very expensive road-cosy. When the lease came up for renewal I decided to bid farewell to my faithful friend. The lease company said it had found a good home for him, in the country with a family who loved taking him for a run, getting his paint scratched by nettles for the first time. I'd only ever been able to scratch him in the BBC car park, where pillars had a habit of unexpectedly appearing when you reversed.

I've had a car ever since I passed my test in 1986. (It was my third or fourth attempt. The examiners knew me by name.) I wondered how I would cope without it.

Six months on, I am coping perfectly well, thank you very much. Not difficult, given I'm lucky enough to live in a city with great public transport, and I'm lucky enough to be able to afford to use it. Giving up a car, I know, is not an option for millions of people who might want to.

Here are the things I don't miss about having a car. Sitting endlessly in traffic. Standing on windy petrol forecourts watching the pence indicator rise so fast it's imperceptible to the human eye. Going to tyre specialists to be told – every time – that every tyre must be replaced or you will certainly die if you dare get behind the wheel again.

The thing I hope I never have to do again for as long as I live is: take the car to the garage for a service. The lease company always insisted I went to a recommended (i.e., expensive) place miles from anywhere. It was always big and glassy, like a Norman Foster airport terminal. They actually employed people wearing headsets and carrying clipboards to greet you as you drove up. They would point earnestly to the car park five yards ahead. Another person would greet you as you emerged from the vehicle and walk with you the ten yards to the doors of the space-age building where the receptionist would take your details for a third time, and offer beverages. I'm not making this up. I've been to less well-staffed, less well-appointed spas.

Thus dropping off the car was always a dreamlike experience. Nothing was too much trouble. But every time the dreamy car people would always turn into the worst wide-boy nightmares. The cheery receptionist was suddenly brusque on the phone. The friendly chap who'd given me his business card and begged to allow him to do anything to help was suddenly *always* on a call and would never return mine. Faults went unfixed, new ones created. And although giant posters from head office pledged unbeatable customer care, no one seemed to care at all. I always came away feeling wretched.

This happened with several makes of car over many years. Was I just unlucky or do big, shiny garages stink?

2015

X is for idiots

I'm terrified of spoiling my postal vote

There are only 6347 more campaigning days left until the election – or so it would seem. But be brave of heart. At some point – possibly after scientists have cured every known disease and we've successfully colonised Neptune – it will be over and we'll have the chance, at last, to vote. The following day, campaigning begins for 2020. It's almost enough to have you googling 'benefits of dictatorship'.

I have mixed feelings about the act of voting. I no longer go to the local polling station on account of complaints from the staff. Unaccountably, they took exception to my well-intentioned attempt to alleviate their monotony by emerging from behind the booth curtain dressed as a clown. Judging from the stream of vituperative letters pouring from the local council's legal department, coulrophobia is rife among polling station personnel. Who knew?

Free citizens of the United Kingdom can apparently vote for clowns, but not vote as them. I wouldn't mind, but the costume was not cheap. I managed to sell most of it to Huw Edwards, who promised to wear it on his last day on the *Ten* if he wins the Lottery, but the shoes were murder to shift. In the end Corrie Corfield took them free of charge. At least they'll fit her.

Postal voting terrifies me. A lot of clever people have spent a lot of time carefully designing the form to ensure they're idiot-proof and yet somehow I struggle.

As I recall from last time, there is a page of instructions, two envelopes including the one it all arrived in, and various flaps and perforations. To my mind, a perforated form is crying out to be teased apart. Not to do so would be like leaving bubble wrap unpopped. But the uncompromising instructions insist you must NOT tear the perforation or your vote might not count.

Signatures must go only in a specified place or your vote might not count. Do NOT put the identity form in the same sub-envelope as the actual voting slip or your vote might not count. Ensure the completed form is placed with the council's address visible in the envelope window and not your own address or your vote might not count. It's all very tense. There is, I think, a phone number you can call if you make a mistake and need new paperwork, but I suspect it's just a recorded message saying 'We made these forms idiot-proof and you still screwed it up. We're taking away your vote. Idiot.'

The business of choosing a candidate is a cinch compared with the tension of preparing all the postal paperwork. Being an unbiased BBC person, I put a cross next to all the names to demonstrate fairness.

The perils of postal voting came back to me this morning when, in advance of a medical examination, I was sent very similar-looking pieces of paper and cardboard, for the collection and storage of three separate – ahem – 'samples'. I stared at the lengthy instructions and jaunty drawings of a stick figure on a lavatory (how would that work?) and had a panic about making a mess of my mess. The humiliation of spoiling a soiling would have been too much.

I correctly put all the envelope A stuff into packet B — though now I think about it, I'm worried I've posted it to Huw Edwards and kept a clown costume for my doctor.

21–27 February

Seeing stars

A postcard from Palm Springs

Greetings from the United States, where I'm holidaying with my good friend, the NBC *Nightly News* anchor Brian Williams. Over a lot of drinks one evening, I shared with Brian some of the tall tales I've told in this column over the years — including that I'd stopped drinking, met Larry Hagman and won the Derby.

He put his arm around me and said, 'Eric, old buddy, that's nothing.' I'm forbidden from passing on his big fib due to the Presenters' Code of Silence, which also precludes me from revealing which big-time BBC News presenter is secretly bald; even her make-up ladies don't know. But if it ever comes out, boy is Brian in trouble.

National treasure

A few days in the warmth of Palm Springs. It's very showbiz. Nowhere else can drivers slip quietly up Kirk Douglas or go down on Bob Hope. On Palm Canyon Drive they have their own selection of stars studded into the sidewalk: a bit like Hollywood, but these names all have a Palm Springs connection, apparently.

There's Victoria Principal, much missed as *Dallas*'s Pamela Barnes Ewing ('Power, money, and control mean nothing to me. I want a nice, ordinary life with my husband') and Leslie Nielsen, much missed on account of being dead ('The truth hurts . . . maybe not as much as jumping on a bicycle with the seat missing, but it hurts.') And there's Carol Channing. She is described on her Palm Springs star as 'Broadway/Movie/ Television/Humanitarian'.

While some readers might have to google Ms Channing, those of us of a certain vintage and inclination will not need reminding that, at the age of ninety-four, she has been a star on stage and screens of all sizes for longer than most of us have been alive. I'm not going to quibble with the idea that she is also a humanitarian – I'm really not. But seeing that word on her star (as Brian and I sashayed down the street, hammered, exchanging stories of our days as astronauts) made me wonder what a humanitarian is. Is it the new national treasure? To qualify, must you repeatedly help the infirm across the road? Donate your salary to good causes? Be photographed donating a tiny proportion of your salary to good causes? I need to know because my Palm Springs star, when it is inevitably cemented in, MUST read: 'Eddie Mair, Radio/ TV/Broadway/Humanitarian/*Celebrity Big Brother* Runner-Up 2039'.

Let there be light

In Palm Springs the street lighting is so minimal the clear night skies reveal the universe in all its glory. In the neighbourhood where I'm renting a place there are no street lights, only car headlights or the occasional porch light to guide you on your way. And I can attest to how amazing the Palm Springs heavens are, after tripping over a fire hydrant and seeing them after I landed flat on my back.

Dressing down

The Palm Springs Aerial Tramway whisks visitors eight thousand feet from desert to mountains in just over ten minutes. They say it's the only place on Earth to experience such a quick temperature change, from 25°C to below freezing, but they've never had a dressing down from the *PM* editor.

14–20 March

Haunted House

The ghost of Auntie Beeb is stalking me

There has been some talk about the state of New Broadcasting House, the billion-pound conservatory added to the back of the Art Deco thirties construction. I say conservatory but that doesn't convey the full grandeur of the project. Try to envisage a cosy ground-floor studio flat with a Sir Norman Foster-designed airport terminal bolted on.

Judging by reports, parts of the new building are falling off, there is a lingering smell akin to a welder's jockstrap and a grey lady stalks the corridors, wailing and gibbering, rattling chains. That last one is certainly true. I've been in her office.

I have seen scant evidence of crumbling edifices, and those that do exist are always quickly and brilliantly restored by make-up artists. The only foul smells are those you'd encounter in any building: occasionally from the loos, and from any meeting with 'ideas' on the agenda.

My concern is something else: the very audible eerie wail that can be heard in the original ship-shaped Broadcasting House. Before you ask, the wailing cannot possibly come from the real-life crazy grey lady, since it also appears after 5.30 p.m. and at weekends.

Coming down some of the beautiful stairwells in BH you will sometimes catch the almost musical note. It's the wind, of course, howling around the miles of corridors, sneaking in and out of musty old window frames, the ghost of programmes past. Perhaps it was another genius part of the design: when the wind catches old BH at a certain angle and speed, you'll imagine you are at sea.

The wailing is intermittent: you can go weeks without hearing it – like the shipping forecast. But I fancy that down the decades my long-gone elders and betters in broadcasting, trudging to the exit after their own radio triumphs and tragedies, also enjoyed the rapture of a building that was dedicated to sound, making one of its own.

I felt like a thief

Theft from stores on what remains of the high street apparently costs the shops, and ultimately us, squillions of pounds a year. Part of their weaponry against shoplifters and dodgy staff is to festoon garments and gizmos with anti-theft devices. At the till, harassed and often poorly paid shop staff will spend aeons trying to locate all the devices before setting you free with your receipt towards the exit.

I don't know about you but when the alarm sounds and

the lights flash a guard often appears and shepherds me back to the desk. He stands over me, menacingly, as the assistant searches endlessly for the sensor she failed to locate. After it's found, there is not a word of apology. No 'I'm sorry our mistake made you look like a thief' or 'Perhaps you have better things to do than spend the entire afternoon in our store'. Would a 'Thank you for your patience' really kill them?

On exiting the store a second time the non-speaking security guard looks at me as if I've been lucky to get away with something this time but he's definitely going to keep an eye out for me and he never forgets a face.

In future, when alarms sound and the lights flash I'm just going to keep walking. If they want to check my bag so badly they can damn well come and get it.

4–10 April

Pain in Spain

How do you silence a busker?

There is much to recommend about the Spanish city of Córdoba. The Mosque–Cathedral is a (World Heritage) sight to behold. Do have a stroll around the Alcázar de los Reyes Cristianos, which my translation app tells me is Abanazar of the Lost Cristiano Ronaldo: there are beautiful gardens. Oh, and there's an exquisite bridge, the name of which I can't recall but you'll know it when you see it.

The old town is expansive and best not attempted in high heels (not the first time I've made that costly error). It is endlessly beguiling. There is nothing I would not recommend about the Andalusian gem that is Córdoba.

Except this: during my visit, as my calves groaned from negotiating the cobbles, I happened upon a picturesque square. The afternoon sun peeked between some of the three- or four-storey white-painted buildings, with their colourful shutters in various states of repair. At street level, cafés and restaurants with tables outside, and a violinist setting up to serenade us all. It felt like the perfect break in the most perfect day. I settled at a table that would soon catch the sun, and an amiable waitress tolerated my terrible Spanish. As I say, perfect.

Then Screech started playing his violin.

You may well have your own pet sounds that have you instantly covering your ears. Fingernails down a blackboard? The yapping of a diminutive dog? An announcer intoning 'It's five o'clock and time for *PM* with Eddie Mair'? I used to love hearing the violin but this chap in Córdoba had a way with the instrument that suggested it had done him some wrong.

I suppose there's a risk with any street artist that their style will not match your mood. If you're in a foul temper, don't head for Covent Garden in London because the chirpy jugglers, comedians, musicians – or, if you're very unlucky, all three in one person – will push you over the edge. Similarly, a clarinettist outside a railway station giving you her 'Stranger on the Shore' is probably the last thing you want to hear if you've just missed the last train. And I could happily go to my grave without hearing another zither piped through a bad PA system in a shopping mall. Generally, though, musicians out of doors hit the spot and add to the gaiety of the nation.

I tried to be charitable as this violinist assaulted a number of classics. He may have been one of Spain's millions of unemployed people and needed the money. Perhaps he was just learning the instrument. We all have to learn.

But I, and judging by the wider responses in the square, everyone else, considered the racket to be a tuneless intrusion. It was very loud, very screechy. No one applauded at the end of any number for fear of encouraging him. The blessed moment of calm between 'tunes' was a thrill, only to be shattered as he attacked another hit from the seventies. On and on it went, filling the square with awfulness.

I had finished my main course, while googling 'ear plugs, Spain' on my mobile, when there was a tap on my shoulder. It was the violinist, looking for money.

I was torn. If I gave him some, would it encourage him to stay? If I didn't, would he stick around and torture us further?

In the end, I gave him a single euro. A sort of compromise. No one else gave him anything.

And he stayed to play his repertoire again.

2–8 May

Tell it straight

We're all sick of waffling politicians

Is this the most stage-managed general election in living memory? I will be revealing my thoughts on this subject at a special news conference where I'll be taking pre-vetted questions only from fully paid-up members of the Eddie Mair Fan Club. In the likely event that he has once again been detained under the Mental Health Act, I will allow one question from the editor of *Bunty*, but absolutely no follow-ups.

I have some sympathy for politicians who turn up to be interviewed on the radio at election time. They're fighting for their livelihoods and futures, and have only a few minutes in which to present their parties in the best possible light.

I suspect some have been advised to use interviews to 'get their message across'. Mmmmm. Posters, leaflets and Party Election Broadcasts are for getting the message across. Interviews ought to be about allowing your policies and arguments to be independently tested.

Long before the campaign started (if you can imagine such a time in human history), *PM* took a deeper interest in the state of our democracy. In the wake of Russell Brand and Jeremy Paxman's thoughtful interventions on whether any of us should take part in this fandango, we asked our audience for ideas on how to tart up the democratic process. I don't think we phrased it quite that way but you get my drift.

The response was enormous. People care about this; don't let anyone tell you otherwise. Hundreds, if not thousands, of people contributed ideas. And in January we asked: how do you want us to cover the election? What would be most useful? Again, a deluge of insights. If our inbox is any guide, people care about the democratic process. They want it to work better.

There were two recurring themes. First, listeners wanted to be told about the parties' policies and then have well-informed experts assess them. On *PM* we're doing that most evenings. The team from Radio 4's *More or Less* are analysing the numbers; Tim Harford memorably described some rather fuzzy figures as 'politicians' maths'. And in a series called 'I Can't ... ' we are hearing from listeners who are struggling to do something (such as getting broadband, a train to work, or buying a house) and Anne McElvoy from *The Economist* is dissecting what the parties might do to help.

The second thing listeners insisted we do is try to hold politicians to account. They told us they were fed up with waffle and questions being ignored. I'm not kidding – quite a few wanted us to ring a bell when waffling started, and several wanted us to bring to a grinding halt any interview where obfuscation was taking place. The degree of fed up-ness was surprising to me. Maybe I and others have been letting them down.

And so during this campaign I'm trying to be especially diligent. It's generally OK: the best politicians are happy to engage, even with my dumbass questions. But one or two seem to have been on bad media training courses and truly believe they can get round honest enquiries about manifesto promises by imitating a speak-your-weight machine. Just brazen it out until the end of the interview . . . until the end of the news cycle . . . until the end of the campaign.

Gloriously, I get paid no matter how much they ignore the questions asked on behalf of the listeners. But how do they think voters feel?

16–22 May

Pesto and me

The real story behind our new chat show

I recently revealed the origins of a ground-breaking, agenda-setting, mind-boggling, ear-popping, bed-wetting series coming up next month on Radio 4. It will feature everyone's favourite mop-headed economics wonk, Robert W. Peston (I'm forbidden from revealing what the W stands for, but it's exactly what you think it is) and beloved broadcaster Me.

As previously discussed, I'm doing this series under duress, so please understand that I share the misgivings I know are already rumbling around your innards and threatening to release themselves in an almighty unwelcome belch of warm air – or, as Robert calls it, analysis.

The original idea, if I can call it that, was quite simply for Robert and me to interview a different person each week. Sometimes the most brilliant ideas are the most straightforward. And then there was this particular idea: take two of the most annoying people on air and make an innocent party respond to their inane witterings.

Someone at Radio 4, no doubt with the word 'Creative' in their job title, must have been over- or under-medicated one morning and decided the world really needed to hear this.

We have had, I kid you not, only one production meeting at which Robert and I were both present. He's very difficult to pin down, but if Giant Haystacks was still alive I'd pay a lot of money to see him give it a go. Robert's suggestions for guests all seemed to be the likes of serving prime ministers or people who'd be even less likely to agree to appear. Mine, as you'd expect, were for surviving *Carry On* stars.

As the deadline for actually doing some work on the series approached, someone had the 'blow me down, this is incredible' idea of adding a twist. It's been decided that Robert and I will each get to choose three guests for the planned six-week series, but we'll be kept in the dark about the other's choices until the recording.

That's right. In week one, Robert will have spent an age preparing to interview his special guest, but the first I'll know about their identity will be when the guest comes into the studio to sit down. In week two, the mitten will be on the other hand, or something.

Next week I will tell you about my efforts to discover who is on his guest list. It's harder than you might imagine to bribe a BBC producer.

*

I can reveal two other things. One: there are whispers that the new show will be *such* an event, Robert and I will feature on the cover of *Radio Times*. Possibly those collectable *Doctor Who*-style covers, with me on one and Robert on the other; in all likelihood a fold-out cover so all his hair can be seen.

Two: the name of the new series. This was something of a tussle between our two giant egos, but candidly, the name really doesn't matter to me, it's the content that matters, surely? Not whatever fancy title we've given it.

Anyway, it'll be called *The Robert Peston Interview Show (with Eddie Mair)*.

Mind the manners

One of the Tube lines in London has replaced the man saying 'Please mind the gap between the train and the platform' with a different man saying 'Mind the gap between the train and the platform'. Why?

30 May–5 June

Mint and jojoba

The day I smelt Robert Peston's hair

The Council Chamber at Broadcasting House in London is an intimidating room. Forget the dazzling designs and glass-panelled meeting rooms you see in *W1A*: the Council Chamber is the heart of the ship-shaped vessel the BBC has sailed in at Portland Place almost since those letters were put together. It's old. Old with a capital O. It smells of history.

The oddly shaped room (close to the bow of the BBC ship) is dominated by a portrait of Lord Reith, above a clock and a fireplace. The chamber was once used for meetings of BBC governors and other grandees. These days it hosts leaving bashes (rather a lot lately) and *Radio Times* photoshoots. More of that in a moment.

The Old BBC Broadcasting Equipment and Memories website has archive photos and describes how splendid the Council Chamber is: a 'dignified room intended for meetings of bodies such as the BBC's Advisory Council, and enabling, for instance, representative international committees to meet in London under the BBC's own roof. Like the Entrance Hall below it, the Council Chamber was designed by the architect of the building, Val Myer . . . It was panelled in light-brown Tasmanian oak. The tables were of Queensland walnut and shaped to follow the curves of the room. The room was illuminated by lamps hidden in wrought-oak urns . . . The curtains were in Chelsea Stripe, a fabric also used in the Concert Hall Green Room.'

Another lovely detail: 'The Council Chamber hosted bridge players in February 1939 and was damaged when a landmine exploded in Portland Place on December 8th, 1940.' Or, as I said: Old.

How things have changed. Yesterday, Robert Peston and I stumbled into this ornate and historic enclosure to have our photos taken for *Radio Times* in order to promote our forthcoming Radio 4 series, *The Robert Peston Interview Show (with Eddie Mair)*. *RT* asked that we turn up looking reasonably smart and be prepared to interview each other. Robert apparently thought he didn't need to wear a tie.

You won't believe how many people it takes to organise a *Radio Times* photoshoot. I counted about fifty, forty-five of whom were hair consultants for Robert. Two people, hired directly from Polyfilla, had the task of making me look younger. The lighting director, tasked with finding a photogenic shot of us both, complained there 'wasn't a wattage low enough', whatever that means.

Robert and I were asked to lark around, with me being 'disruptive'. I was allowed to touch Robert's glasses (he slightly bristled) and stood so close to him I could smell his shampoo (mint and jojoba?). At one stage I even accidentally touched his famous hair with an index finger. I noticed this morning that my fingerprint has vanished.

Then we took turns interviewing each other. The questions included: would you interview Boris Johnson again; did you always know you were gay; and what happened to the *Newsnight* gig? I can't remember what Robert asked me.

If the press regulator doesn't ban the article and photographs on the grounds of them being a crime against humanity, you'll be able to see them in a forthcoming edition. Be warned: I swear I saw Lord Reith cover his eyes.

4–10 July

Jurassic bike

My madcap London dash to see dinosaurs

My apologies to all road users between BBC Broadcasting House and the Odeon at Whiteleys in London last Tuesday. What you had to endure was unforgivable but I hope a word of explanation might placate you, although I realise the sight you saw you'll carry with you to the grave. It happened like this, you see.

Paddy O'Connell and I had booked tickets for *Jurassic*

World. After a typical day at the BBC you want something to take your mind off work, although in the end, decent people being eaten alive by heartless monsters running amok proved no distraction.

How I curse our decision to demur from the 9 p.m. screening. That would have given us oodles of time for the journey, and time for oodles of noodles at a well-known Chinese establishment in the Bayswater Road. But as we advance into our autumn years, I think I can speak for us both when I say that the 9 p.m. showing of anything is now a thing of the past for Paddy and me. Who can stay awake? That'll get me home *when*?

The 6.35 it was, then. In days gone by we would simply have done what we always did: flag down a taxi and charge it to the *Farming Today* account. Or, better still, drag up, leap in the back of the official *Woman's Hour* stretch limo and demand in a falsetto that the driver put his bally foot down. Sadly those days of BBC profligacy are over, and quite right too of course, though I do think Lord Hall personally frisking all staff as they leave to check for petty pilfering is a bit much. I suppose it stems from the day Kirsty Wark made it out of Broadcasting House with an American-style fridge under her anorak.

With few other options, we opted to cycle to the cinema. Why not? Paddy has a bike of his own and I could rent one from one of the many cycle-hire stations that festoon London. We'd be at the cinema in no time.

Paddy was waiting for me as I emerged from that night's *PM*, bleeding as per. His bike is manly in every respect. Not only that, it has a prominent frontal basket, which he assures me makes it invisible to the city's bike thieves. I duly hired my bicycle and off we went.

As we wobbled gamely into the traffic, it occurred to us

that we had not discussed a route. Our general sense of direction was fine but which of these streets would get us there? Vehicles in the Marylebone area were treated to ageing gentlemen bellowing directions at each other inaudibly against the traffic noise. Which street was best? Paddy would wildly gesticulate that going up George was wise, while my hands clearly indicated a desire to explore Robert Adam. 6.35 comes and goes.

Both a little puffed, we made it to the halfway point, having agreed it was fine for bikes to go the wrong way down one-way streets (twice). Tourists take photos. Cars toot. A dead end foxes us momentarily but we dismount and push in a genteel fashion. Picture Joan Hickson's Marple, sweating.

At last, the cinema on Bayswater Road is ahead and to the right, though a No Right Turn sign has other ideas. Obviously, Paddy and I did *not* do an illegal manoeuvre. We made it for the start of the film. Two old dinosaurs.

18–24 July

Demon barber

My quest for a quick short back 'n' sides

If there's one thing you can say about my hair, it's that it never gets intertwangled. The individual hairs on my head are so far apart they've got different postcodes. My bald spot is so large midwives use its dimensions to indicate when dilation is complete. I have a letter from Relate confirming that, try as they might, even they could not get my hairs any closer together.

I've long since accepted this as a fact of life, in the same way I accept I will never be a tightrope walker (don't have the head for heights), a prima ballerina (don't have the legs for tights) or host international boxing matches in my back garden (don't have the shed for fights).

So you will be as shocked as I was by a recent visit to a barber's in a strange place. Let's call it Brighton — for that's where it was.

I have a fondness for getting my hair cut when I travel. In part this is because I'm banned from most local hairdressers because of my insistence on hogging the drier for hours at a time (I really just like my chats with the girls).

But whenever I'm abroad, a haircut is a great way to interact with the locals and, given my rudimentary follicular demands, I can make my needs known in any language. I've been trimmed and groomed all over the world and only once did I get in any bother: I told a Fox News-viewing barber in America's Deep South that I worked for the BBC.

I was early for a meeting in the aforementioned city (and Hove) and so with twenty minutes to kill I popped into a friendly-looking barber shop in The Lanes. I was seated right away by a chatty chappie who got to work immediately tracking down my hair and making it slightly shorter. In no time he'd informed me of upcoming local events, his excitement about his new girlfriend and how she'd been accepted by his family, who it turns out had never really liked that bitch of an ex-wife of his, and their planned holiday the next day to somewhere sunny. Him and the new girlfriend, not the ex-wife.

I didn't like to look at my watch for fear of indicating boredom but I was aware that time was passing. He didn't cut at the same speed as he chatted. Other patrons were coming and going from adjacent seats, but I was still there, being mercilessly trimmed by the world's smallest scissors. I could feel my phone throb, no doubt with messages from my friend wondering why I was late. How late was I?

You'll have heard how broadcasters sometimes dare each other to include a certain word or phrase in a programme, just for a giggle. I began to speculate as to whether barbers had private side bets about how long they could detain the almost bald when they come in for a trim. Was I the subject of a colossal in-joke?

Having fully briefed me on all aspects of his life, the barber finally freed me from his clutches. I looked at my watch. Fifty minutes had passed since I sat down for a dry cut, no wash. I was thirty minutes late for my meeting.

In my hurry to exit, wishing chatty chappie a happy holiday, I left the biggest tip I've ever left sober, fearful of a ten-minute hunt for change.

And when I arrived for the meeting I was told in no uncertain terms that I was late and my hair was a mess.

8–14 August

Brits abroad

How to make an exhibition of yourself

Expos, or to use their more elegant title, World's Fairs, can trace their roots back to London in 1851. Bully for them. For reasons best known to themselves, this year's event is being staged inside a furnace. Well, that's how Milan in July felt to me; your experience may differ.

I'd never been to an Expo before, but finding myself for a day en route to the Alps, I hurried through some of the city's other attractions to get there. (My potted reviews: Milan Cathedral – big. Queue to see *The Last Supper* – bigger.)

I had no idea what an Expo would entail. Drawings of the 1851 Crystal Palace/Hyde Park bash suggested I could expect an old queen with a Prince Albert but I was in no mood for that kind of thing. You could buy tickets for a three-day visit but, with my time limited, I opted to pop in for an afternoon.

The scale of it is somewhat daunting. The entrance plaza alone is the size of Kent. I think Expo is Italian for enormous. Once inside, I wandered into the nearest aircraft hangar-sized building in search of air-conditioning and found a baffling exhibition, the purpose of which I cannot describe to you. There were helpful signs describing what we could see but they appeared to have been written and approved by a committee of well-meaning international diplomats, then proof-read by anxious lawyers. I've read BBC memos that made more sense.

I found the exit and headed back into the oven that was the great outdoors, and made my way to the main boulevard, a wide, vehicle-free street lined with the flags of almost every nation, as far as the eye could see. Each flag denoted the site of that nation's pavilion. Each pavilion was the size of Selfridges, or so it seemed as I began the long walk down one side of the street. I suddenly understood why it could take three days.

Leaving aside the disappointing realisation that my knowledge of world flags is not what it was when I was nine, I was struck by several things. There was no queue outside the UK pavilion, which was sad because we're known for that kind of thing. In contrast, there was a huge line of people waiting to enjoy Kazakhstan. Mind you, they had laid on entertainment (a spirited woman singing and dancing with gusto) and were spraying the dehydrated queuers with water. Why didn't we think of that?

The British pavilion had a bee theme (I detect the hand of Martha Kearney – words I haven't used since the Christmas party) and served Pimm's and fish and chips. My visits to other pavilions were limited by queuing and fatigue. Japan, China, the US and South Korea had hundreds of people lining up to sample their delights but I had no time, opting instead for unpopular pavilions such as those for the regions of Italy. Lombardy's effort consisted of a small room with some chairs and a video wall showing aerial shots of Lombardy. What a thrill.

Like going to the dentist and one season of the Robin Pesto show, I'm glad I did it but wouldn't want to do it again. If it's your kind of thing, book now for Expo 2017 in Kazakhstan. I hear the singing, dancing and tourist hydration there are wonderful.

5–11 September

Eddie the idiot

Whoops! I've put my foot in it again

Recently, I recorded an interview for *iPM* with a young woman who's been living with anorexia for many years. She'd just become a 'free-range' human being again, as she put it, having been sectioned under the Mental Health Act for months. She'd been close to death more than once. We spent an hour in conversation. Her mother was by her side, contributing her own experience. They were both unflinching and entirely admirable for having come through their respective traumas. Not for the first time in my line of work, I was impressed by the interviewees' good humour in the face of what life had thrown at them. This was amply demonstrated just before we started our conversation.

As you may know, it's quite normal, prior to a recording, for the host and guest to provide 'sound level'. By saying a few random words before the interview proper, we can be sure everyone's voices can be heard from the start. There's a number of stock questions people like me will ask a guest in those circumstances. Over the years I've asked guests to give me their full names and job titles, or describe how they got to the studio, or give me a burst of 'Peter Piper Picked . . .'

There are so many to choose from. I've done it thousands of times. On this particular morning, with this astonishingly brave mother and daughter sitting opposite me, expectant and perhaps a little nervous, I somehow manage to choose another stock sound-level phrase. I heard myself saying to the young woman, 'Tell me what you had for breakfast.'

I can tell you conclusively now that there is no God. Had He or She existed, the ground would indeed have swallowed me up, as per my instant request. No sooner were the words out of my mouth than I flushed like an Armitage Shanks convention. The floor appeared to give way in what I imagined at first was part of the Good Lord's Quick Response Unit. But no, I was still sitting there and the young woman was still opposite me. Without missing a beat, and apparently unfazed by the presenter turning redder than a sunburnt Jeremy Corbyn supporter, she answered my question.

I blurted out that the breakfast question was something I often asked, and said I hoped she hadn't been offended. She smiled and waved away my protestations and we quickly moved on. If I'd caused offence, she didn't show it: the same good grace she displayed when the interview proper began. My heart rate calmed down to about seven hundred beats per minute and I mentally prepared to compose yet another letter of complaint to an antiperspirant manufacturer.

Update: is Pesto leaving?

I was shocked to read in a recent *Radio Times* that the BBC's economics editor Rabin Prescott is in talks to become the political editor of ITV News. So shocked that I asked Mr Prestonpans about it live on air on *PM*. It was an arresting moment as he reached for what sounded to me like a non-denial denial.

If he leaves the BBC, it will indeed be a tragedy. For ITV. And you can be sure I will be asking him about it when we appear together, as we're contractually obliged to, at this month's *Radio Times* Festival jamboree. I will not be asking him for voice level, however.

19–25 September

Pesto and me live

The Radio Times *Festival is coming soon . . .*

This will be my last column before the *Radio Times* Festival. I am taking the whole of next week off just to prepare for an event that's so big, so . . . everywhere, that it makes Christmas look like a whelk stall.

If you're unaware of the Festival, then let me be the first to congratulate you for emerging successfully from that coma. At the end of September, at the very point in the calendar where none of us knows whether to dress for winter yet, thousands of people will converge on a purpose-built palace in London to celebrate all that is wonderful about broadcasting.

I have *begged* the *Radio Times* people to mention the Festival somewhere in the magazine, to give you some clue as to what it's all about, and I hope to goodness they've taken my advice. The three questions I'm most often asked in the street are: 'When is the *Radio Times* Festival?', 'How do I get tickets for the *Radio Times* Festival?' and 'Why don't you pick up that bonnet, put down that penny whistle, stop begging for change and get a real job?'

I'm thrilled to say I will be in attendance, signing copies of my new book, *Robert Peston: My Part in his Downfall*. It's a controversial unauthorised warts-and-all biography, which has already been lambasted by critics for spending three chapters discussing Robert's warts. But I say to them: when you've spent as long as I have in radio studios listening to Robert talk, you do search around for something – anything – to distract you from what he's actually saying.

So I have become something of an authority on the cauliflower-shaped growths on his never-done-a-day's-work-in-his-life hands. The critics can scoff. I have already sold the film rights to Robert's life story. Robert is being a touch precious about finding the right actor to play him, Omar Sharif having recently died, but I can tell you the film will have a PG certificate.

I will be taking part in a number of sessions at the Festival. On opening night, this Thursday, it's me inside that gorilla costume stalking Sir David Attenborough as he discusses six decades in broadcasting. On the Friday I'm in charge of the lights for the session hosted by BBC Radio's Head of Director of In Charge of Radio, Dame Helen Boaden, entitled 'Radio in the Dark'.

On the Saturday please do not miss the event in which I discuss my hitherto secret role behind the scenes in shepherding *Call the Midwife* to our screens. I'll also be hosting a session featuring some of the stars of *The Archers*, and will be sitting down with Mr Pesto for an hour of riveting and lively conversation.

In all candour, I have no idea what we will do for the hour. My guess is it will be like our recent Radio 4 interview programme, the title of which matters not one whit, which was essentially a Robert monologue with occasional interruptions. If I wasn't already booked to be in it, I'd be buying tickets to see it.

On the Sunday there is a session hosted by my agent of thirty-five years (our time together, not her age), Anita Land. The niece of Lew Grade, she looks back at the archive of a whole evening of ITV programming from one night in 1964, which the impresario arranged to have recorded for posterity. An interesting event in and of itself, and for me, a chance to finally meet her.

17–23 October

I'm not dead yet

Stairlifts can wait until I'm fifty-one

And so it begins. I will be fifty years old next month. I'm approaching my half-century in the same way I used to approach working with Robert Peston: close my eyes and just try to get through it without having a breakdown. There will be no fuss, no flowers, perhaps a little light catering: a bit like my own funeral plans. In fact, if I threw in an open wicker

casket for my fiftieth, it would be *exactly* like my funeral plans.
I'll talk to the birthday caterers.

The point is, as it approaches, I'm not terribly fussed about
it. Perhaps when it arrives it will hit me like Joan Collins in
practically any season of *Dynasty*, but for now I am serene like
Barbara Bel Geddes in practically any season of *Dallas* (except
1984/85, of course).

That was until yesterday when, with weeks to go before
the day I am completely calm about, an email arrived out of
the blue. I'm going to quote directly from it. Be prepared to
be shocked. 'Hello, Over 50 and looking for life insurance?
[Name of insurance company] Guaranteed Over 50s Life
Insurance can help give you peace of mind by providing a
benefit amount for your loved ones if you were to pass away,
to help pay for your funeral, any final expenses or to leave
your family a cash gift. £2,000 to £15,000 benefit amount
depending on your age. For all UK residents aged 50 to 79.
Immediate cover for accidental death. After 12 months you
are covered for death by any cause.'

How do they get away with this? Is this legal? Why aren't
the police arresting these people?

Here I am in my prime, still technically in my forties, and
they're calling the funeral directors! Wait – maybe the funeral
directors will be next in my inbox with some enticing offer.
'Act now to get our bargain rates. Don't wait until you're in
your mid-fifties. Die now, you pointless old sod.'

And this is just the start. How long until I'm being enticed
onto cruises? Being offered pens just for applying for funeral
plans? Slip-free shower mats, stairlifts, high-waist elasticated
trousers and cash-in-your-pension-quick schemes? There's
nothing wrong with any of these things. Some even seem
quite attractive now, especially those practical trews. But
really, please, give me a break. Wait until I'm fifty-one.

Well, let me see the brochure for the shower mats and I'll have a think. Easy payment plan, you say?

Farewell, Pesto

I've been asked to say a few words about Rabbiting Pressman, my BBC colleague who is about to become an ITV person. Of course I could write a few platitudes about wishing him well, thanking him for our glorious time together on *PM* and that interview show whose title I can never remember. I could get deadly serious and intone that, for all our joshing and feuding, he was like a brother to me, and I'm going to miss him with all my heart. But that wouldn't really be in keeping with the tone of our relationship.

What I'd like to do is quote something from our last session together, at the *Radio Times* Festival, when Rabbit and I answered questions from the great-looking audience. This actually happened in response to a person who asked about Rabbie's distinctive broadcasting style:

Robin: 'I'm the Marmite of broadcasters.'

Me: 'But some people like Marmite.'

7–13 November

Dallas revisited

The week I struck Ewing oil

Dateline: Dallas, Dealey Plaza, 2015. I appreciate that, journalistically, it would have been more exciting to have been here fifty-two years ago, but I wasn't born then. This is my second visit to the site where JFK was assassinated by Lee Harvey Oswald/a man wearing a police uniform on the grassy knoll/the mafia/the CIA/the Cubans/the Russians/his driver/Sue Ellen's sister, Kristin.

Last time I missed a small but important detail on Elm Street, the three-lane road where the president met his end. In the middle lane, a few yards apart, there are crosses, which appear to mark the very spots where the shots hit their target. Astonishing. No wonder the shooter(s) had no trouble. I can't help thinking that if the Secret Service had done their jobs properly and noticed the crosses before the assassination, things might have turned out more agreeably for everyone. How did Oliver Stone miss them?

I'm visiting this fine city to celebrate my impending fiftieth birthday. Ten years ago, my good friend, television's Richard Arnold, and I marked my last landmark birthday in New York City. Like two characters in a downmarket, poorly scripted film, we vowed that if I survived until my fiftieth (indeed, if we survived the week in New York), we would travel to Dallas together.

Why Dallas, you ask? I've a passing interest in the TV series of the same name. And Richard ... well, if I tell you that *Dallas* was Richard's specialist subject on *Celebrity Mastermind*, you'll have some idea of his passion for the Greatest Primetime Soap in History.

You and I can both name Southfork Ranch as the improbably small home of the Ewing clan, Pam as Bobby's wife and Donna Reed as the unfortunate woman who replaced Barbara Bel Geddes for a season, only to be yanked off screen without so much as a thank you. But Richard's knowledge of *Dallas* is such that if he was that clever about, say, renewable energy or interstellar space travel, the world would be living off power generated by thin air and holidaying on the other side of the universe.

For instance, who said: 'I always get what I want'; 'Dr Elby, he's GOT to be STOPPED!'; or, 'Your own land is the most precious thing you can own'? (Answers: JR in almost every episode; Sue Ellen to her psychiatrist just prior to the second shooting of JR, the first having been with his daddy when they were hunting; Miss Ellie staring out at her beloved ranch.)

We're eating in some of Dallas's finest establishments. No meal is complete without Richard referring to the waiting staff by the names of characters who used to serve breakfast at Southfork or drinks at the Cattlemen's Club. The male staff get 'Raoul' and the females 'Cassie'. Why he doesn't get punched more, I don't know. Goodness knows I have tried several times.

A stroll around downtown Dallas is not, on the face of it, the most thrilling experience, but, with *Good Morning Britain*'s showbiz correspondent, it becomes the eighties again. 'Look, it's the Ewing Oil building! Look, it's the Wentworth Tool and Dye building! Look, it's West Star Oil!' It's fun for a while but midweek I am pushing him into the road and saying 'Look, it's a Greyhound bus'. Two minutes in the morning is one thing but a whole week? What was I thinking?

14–20 November

Mrs Elvis and me

The stars of Southfork stalk Dallas

Forgive me, please, for returning to Dallas – but if it's good enough for Bobby Ewing, it's good enough for me. As revealed last week, I've come here with my old pal Richard Arnold to celebrate my fiftieth birthday. Richard is *Good Morning Britain*'s showbiz correspondent or something (I tune him out when he talks about work). He's an even bigger fan than I am of the greatest ever primetime soap, so this was the obvious place for us both to mark my half-century.

Dallas is full of fine hotels . . . But where to stay for a land-mark birthday? We were inspired by Larry Hagman himself. In his autobiography, *Hello Darlin'*, 'Sir' Larry reveals that whenever they were filming in Dallas, he, his wife, Linda Gray and Priscilla Presley stayed at the 'luxurious Mansion on Turtle Creek Hotel, which is one of the three best hotels I've ever been in in my life'.

Well, I didn't need to be asked twice. If it's good enough for Mr and Mrs JR Ewing and Mrs Elvis Presley, it's good enough for me. The Mansion is indeed beautiful, with terrific service and attention to detail. I wish I'd asked for a reduction in the bill in exchange for this glowing review in print, but at checkout time I was involved in a fist fight with Richard, who I swear had promised to foot the bill as a birthday treat.

Down the road is Turtle Creek, and looming over it is an old railway line that's been transformed into a public space for walkers, runners, cyclists and mad skaters. I raved about it to Richard, but I think he tunes me out when I talk about anything.

The trip to Southfork has been the highlight of the visit (with the possible exception of a line-dancing mix-up in a dimly lit bar). Annoyingly, it's not located near downtown Dallas: it's a bit of a schlep out of town to Parker (not only a chauffeur and a pen, but also a city in Collin County, Texas).

Smaller than expected, the inside of this most famous 'Barratt home' was never used for filming and has merely been done up *Dallas*-style. The experiences come alive outside: you can step out on to the balcony, sit by the pool and loiter in the driveway where so many cars screeched to a halt before the driver had a confrontation, usually with JR. And then there are the striped yellow and white awnings. It's like coming home.

The tour guide (corrected by Richard only twice) tells us that the glass table on the patio is the one used for all those windswept, uneaten breakfasts. Do I detect Sue Ellen's spittle? No, it's just a drop of rain. I'll be sorry to leave.

Peter Donaldson – the voice of BBC radio

Last Monday, on what would turn out to be Peter Donaldson's last day, a group of his colleagues from Radio 4 Continuity, past and present, gathered to record a few words about him for broadcast after his death. There were some tears and much sadness, but a lot of laughter too. There was a great deal of love and affection for a breathtakingly good broadcaster, a kind man with a streak of naughtiness, a terrific, supportive boss, and a man who loved the BBC to his core while having a healthy disdain for some of its managerial madnesses. A voice of the network silenced. Thank you, Peter.

5–11 December

My busking hell

Don't go to Barcelona for the music

When I think of Barcelona, I think of sore feet. Not the most romantic thing that's ever been written about the jewel in

Catalonia's crown, but there is a truth to it. Whenever I'm there – as I was recently – there's always a tremendous amount of walking.

The Barça streets invite you to stroll and it's an invitation I never reject. At the end of each visit I feel I must have traversed the entire city, but in reality almost all of it remains unexplored. My feet remove themselves from my legs and soak themselves defiantly in hot water, and I vow that I will take the Metro more next time. But where's the fun in that?

I did pop underground once this time and regretted it. You may recall an incident I recounted in Córdoba, when the peaceful lunch of dozens of holiday-makers in a sun-kissed plaza was ruined by a shambolic violinist. What the violin had done to him, I never found out, but the man was clearly intent on revenge.

Memories of that day came flooding back when the gentle hubbub in my Metro train was shattered by the unmistakable screech of a violin. It was worse than Córdoba for two reasons. His playing was, unbelievably, worse than the other guy's, and he'd taken the trouble to amplify the sound through a tinny speaker. He also had some kind of pre-recorded boop-she-boop backing track. The entire carriage was forced to endure his performance of several barnstorming Spanish standards.

Brilliantly, just when I thought the pain could not get worse, a woman's voice was added to the cacophony. I removed my head from my hands to see what was happening.

The bloke had not only come along with his violin, backing track and speakers, but also a woman who was giving full voice to the classics. No song was safe as she belted them out into her silver microphone – which had all my sympathy, as it was closest to the noise and covered in balladeer spit.

I swear to you there was talk of revolution on the train,

stopped only by the glorious moment the racket finally ceased. In what I took to be an ironic coda to the performance, the woman passed through the carriage shoving an empty Starbucks cup under the noses of passengers. It dawned on me that she must have wanted financial recompense for finally desisting from the song-murdering. When the cup passed in front of me, I gave her a contemptuous look and dropped in the business card of a music teacher acquaintance of mine. I hope she looks him up.

The purpose of the trip – about which more next week – was to celebrate my fiftieth birthday, but I'm happy to tell you even the Med's biggest city couldn't top the thrill of getting a call on the day itself from the one and only Mr Barry Cryer.

'I'm on the train,' his unmistakable voice intoned. 'I read in the paper that you're fifty. I just wanted to say that you don't look it.' (Pause.) 'But you must have done once.'

A call from Barry to politely insult me with a funny joke. Honestly, they could have finished the Sagrada Família on my birthday and it would not have made me happier.

2016

Telling porkies

My humble pie that straddled the world

We've made it nearly to the end of January. Well done, us! I can almost smell February – or it could be the pork pie rotting in my desk drawer. Here at the Broadcasting House Fun Factory it's like a non-stop party. Imagine Lord Hall as Willy Wonka (the Gene Wilder version), and his eager staff as his dedicated Oompa-Loompas. Now you get some idea of the nutty, crazy antics that happen here 24/7. Yes, there are chocolate rivers on every floor, lifts that go sideways and even Wonkavision. Not so long ago there was even a jacuzzi of cash, but Mark Thompson took that with him to the *New York Times*.

I'm terribly sorry – I think I've inhaled some more pie fumes.

The aforementioned delights of the good Lord's broadcasting hub are not in fact as psychedelic as I indicated. Let's just say that the plumbers have promised to fix the chocolate rivers. Similarly, engineers are working on the lifts that move sideways. The unorthodox motion has been handy for moving people who've been unsuccessful at job interviews, but they've caused several coffee-related spillages, and a while ago Alan Yentob got into one and hasn't been seen since. As for Wonkavision – well, it's going 'online only' next month.

However, each floor of Broadcasting House does boast its own fridge or two, where we Oompa-Loompas can store food. It was in our third-floor fridge a few weeks ago that I spied a Co-op pork pie that had a use-by date of 17 November (I assumed 2015). I wondered how long it might sit there before the member of staff who'd bought it remembered it and threw it away.

Days became weeks and still the pie sat, unmoved by the constantly changing landscape around it in the third-floor fridge. Ready meals, bottled water, salads and even mince pies came and went, but the pie did not budge.

Bored one day, I took to photographing it with the masthead of a newspaper, in the style of a ransom demand, then posted the photo on Twitter. I did that for a week before getting bored with that too.

Tweeters wondered what it would taste like. Had our outgoing economics editor Rabbiting Press-on left it as a parting gift? Would it get its own series? It wouldn't be the first thing past its sell-by date to get six weeks out of the BBC.

Then last week an email arrived from a colleague in a part of the BBC empire that was not Broadcasting House. Here is a direct quote from what he sent: 'I wanted you to know the fridges here at the BBC in [redacted] have just been cleared of all out-of-date food by an unhappy man muttering about "some Radio 4 presenter" and a "pork pie". We salute you.'

Incredible, isn't it? A pork pie flaps its wings in a London fridge and a hurricane sweeps through a fridge hundreds of miles away. I've finally achieved something with my life.

PS: A couple of weeks ago, I removed the pie from the fridge and put it in my drawer. When famous faces pass my desk I ask if they'd be willing to be photographed with the pie. I tweeted a photo of Rabbiting Press-on holding the item with the heading 'An out of date #porkpie'.

13–19 February

Don't call me Shirley

Even the best-laid joke can backfire

The BBC's technology correspondent, Rory Cellan-Jones. com, is the man to turn to for answers on anything that needs to be plugged in, or that travels mysteriously through wires or even connects magically without wires. There's nothing he doesn't know. He's half man, half microchip.

At *PM*, where we still struggle with the pencil sharpener, he is the reliable source of knowledge in an ever-changing technological world. What do you know: I read the other day that it will one day be possible to order goods from shops just by using your mobile phone. And get this: SOME OF THE SHOPS WON'T ACTUALLY HAVE SHOPS! I'm giddy – and I don't think it's all down to Martha Kearney's home-made gin that she's insisted I sample. It has quite a kick, and, if I'm not mistaken, a hint of bees.

Where was I? Oh yes – Rory was in the *PM* studio the other night explaining a strange phenomenon whereby news stories that are years out of date are somehow treated as searingly topical. (I could insert a cheap aside here at Robert Peston's expense, but what would be the point?) This particular quirk happens sometimes on the BBC News website, among others. Ancient tales about a man marrying a goat or the deaths of Tony Hart or Leslie Nielsen suddenly end up trending as the most-read topical stories. Rory's explanation live on air was something about chaos theory: a butterfly flaps its wings in Japan and in London the FTSE 100 plunges as if it has an anvil around its neck. Something like that. All very interesting. But it wasn't what we planned.

Leslie Nielsen's most famous role was as Dr Rumack in the spoof air-disaster movie *Airplane!*, in which he was involved in several exchanges that went a bit like this:

Ted Striker: Surely you can't be serious?

Dr Rumack: I am serious. And don't call me Shirley.

We thought it would be a subtle treat for fans of the film if, during Rory's live appearance, we dropped in that kind of exchange. Rory would say something about chaos theory and I would say: 'Surely you can't be serious.' He would deadpan: 'I am serious – and don't call me Shirley.' What a hilarious gift for our discerning listeners. But it didn't work out like that.

While I babbled away on air about something else, Rory appeared in the production cubicle and had a brief chat with the editor. He then headed into the on-air studio and the editor told me in my headphones that she'd reminded him about our affectionate Nielsen tribute. When Rory sashayed in, there was a recorded report playing and I also reminded him about our little plan. He was absolutely happy with it.

And so we were live on air. I introduced the item, explaining the strange internet phenomenon, introduced Rory and asked him what was going on. In due course he came to mention chaos theory. I seized the moment and said my line, but Rory, without missing a beat, carried on as if I hadn't said a word. I gave him my best Paddington hard stare but the opportunity had passed. A moment of radio gold – lost. I fought back tears.

Afterwards, Rory was mortified that it had slipped his

mind. This kind of thing happens, and as yet there isn't an app to stop it.

20–26 February

That was Wogan

Even when all at sea, Sir Terry never faltered

The day after the death of Sir Terry Wogan was announced, *PM* launched Wogan Week. Every night, just before our prestigious closing theme (Big Ben's bongs) we ransacked the archives so we could play different clips illustrating Terry down the years.

Monday was something from perhaps one of his last Radio 2 broadcasts, in November. Tuesday was a confab with Jimmy Young from the mid-eighties; Wednesday brought some fight the flab from Radios 1 and 2 in the early seventies (he sounded even more Irish); Thursday a bit of his Radio 2 breakfast show from 2006; and then the week came to a shuddering climax with an innocent Janet and John tale that inexplicably ended with Sir Terry and his entire presentation team collapsing in giggles. Most unprofessional!

My favourite was Tuesday's clip. Wogan was not in the studio at Broadcasting House – he was in as inhospitable a broadcasting environment as you could get: hundreds of miles away on an oil rig in the North Sea.

Outside broadcasts always present challenges (translation: they can be a pain in the backside). Communications are invariably ropey, and if something can go wrong, it will. I once had to abandon ship in Sydney Harbour when our satellite failed. On an OB of extraordinarily complex technicalities in California, our carefully laid plans were almost ruined when, with less than a minute to go, every single electrical item went dead simultaneously with a terrifying *fzzzzz*. The cause? I had accidentally pulled out the main socket on my way back from a last-minute PTP (pre-transmission pee).

Terry in his chat with Jimmy Young that morning was so focused and sharp you'd have assumed he was in the studio next door. Wogan relentlessly teased and mocked his colleague, sharp as a tack. Jimmy informed him he would be on holiday the following week and asked Wogan to guess who his stand-in would be.

Young: 'Guess who you'll be talking to next week.'

Wogan: 'Em, Diana Dors!'

Young (with a proud theatrical flourish): 'David Frost!'

Wogan (almost before Young had finished speaking): 'Same thing.'

Moments later, from the oil rig, Wogan cued the next piece of music. 'That was Jimmy Young. This is Frank Sinatra … who's not quite as old.' And of course, his quip ended just as Sinatra's vocal started. Perfect.

A big birthday

We did a Peter Allen week once on *PM* – to mark his departure from 5 Live *Drive*. (We've also done a Shatner week, but that's another story.)

As it happens, Peter dropped by the *PM* office last week, clutching a bag with a half-eaten cake in it. If Wogan was the perfect music presenter, Peter may be the perfect news presenter, though I'd never tell him that. Plus he doesn't appear to age and his hair, which makes Boris Johnson's look like a comb-over, is more lustrous than ever.

Peter mumbled something about it being his birthday that very day. We wished him happy birthday and he left the cake for the *PM* team to gorge on, not wanting any fuss.

Only later did we discover that it wasn't just any birthday – it was one with a zero at the end. Many happy returns, Peter Allen.

7–12 May

My last word

Why death and deadlines don't mix

It was Benjamin Franklin who said one day, 'I'm going to think up a really good and enduring quote about death and taxes', and he did, because he was nothing if not a doer. The quote was this: 'In this world nothing can be said to be certain, except death and taxes.' He was wrong about taxes, but then he'd never visited Panama.

In any event, moments before Mr Franklin experienced the truth of his own quiet expiration, on 17 April 1790, he sat bolt upright and said, 'Oh, and referendum campaigns go on too long. I should have said death and taxes and the fact that referendum campaigns go on too long.' And then he died. Sadly, there was no one there to record the event, so we're stuck with the original unamended quote.

Radio 4's *More or Less* recently examined why so many celebrities are dying these days, and concluded that it's because the government is controlling the weather. Or maybe my DAB radio re-tuned during the item, because that doesn't really make any sense. Certainly, the Grim Reaper appears to be on some kind of performance-related bonus package this year.

Death is news and journalists develop a sort of detachment about death. We say it's because becoming emotionally transfixed by each person's passing would stop us doing our jobs properly – a bit like nurses and doctors. I'm not so sure. It may be because we're just not very nice people in the first place. And with the honourable exception of the many journalists who put themselves in harm's way reporting on the world's never-ending supply of wars, I suspect people in the medical profession have more reason to be death-hardened than office-based pen-pushers like me.

Sometimes death is unkind to our deadlines.

Lady Thatcher's death was reported by the Press Association at around 12.50 p.m. In our office, I saw the *World at One* production team leap into action, throwing out their entire running order and somehow mounting a full programme devoted to that one subject.

The news about Victoria Wood's death was reported by the Press Association at 3.14 p.m. At *PM*, we scrambled to put together something meaningful for listeners. Few people returned our calls. Sometimes producers find themselves in the position of telling one celebrity about the death of someone close to them. They do it with great tact, but it's awful nonetheless.

Fewer celebrities want to appear on the radio these days to pay tribute to the recently departed: Twitter is a quicker and easier outlet for them. Melvyn Bragg did a splendid turn for *PM* talking about Victoria Wood, and our ace producers compiled a beautiful montage of her *Desert Island Discs* mixed with some of her writing and performances.

The following night, with two minutes of *PM* left, we saw the American website TMZ reporting Prince's death. We decided not to 'flash' such information without double-checking, but sadly, as you know, they got it right.

By the time this column reaches you other celebs may have passed. I too may die, making this my last ever column. Which makes me wish I had a better ending.

First-class mail

The joys of unsolicited post

In days gone by I could rely on a weekly piece of excitement in the post. No, not my updated copy of *John Whittingdale's Diary* – I'm talking about my subscription edition of *Radio Times*. Before you ask, no, I never got a free subscription.

These days my paid subscription comes via my iPad app, which means that, while I have the full majesty of the magazine wherever I go, I no longer have that satisfying thud on my doormat every Tuesday.

In the past few weeks, though, two items of mail arrived to make up for my aching loss.

The first was voting papers for the recent elections. I'm barred from my local polling station after a misunderstanding on my part of precisely what a spoilt paper was. They dropped the charges after I agreed to postal voting in future and paid for the dry cleaning of the polling-booth curtain.

Inside the envelope there was a piece of paper with a perforation across it, which included an envelope marked A with the words 'Do not tear off this section'. There was a separate piece of paper with instructions on both sides explaining how to vote. There was an envelope marked B (it seems A goes into B, or possibly the other way round) and there were three separate voting slips. One pink, one orange and one yellow.

One was for the London Assembly, one was for the Mayor of London and one was for the post of Election Simplifier. I took great care choosing that one.

The second item of mail was a delightful throwback to days I thought had vanished into history, like Billy Smart's Circus on TV on Christmas Day, or a Bernie Sanders victory.

It was A4-sized and bright orange, with lettering full of urgency, like a wailing burglar alarm in printed form. These are actual quotes: 'ATTENTION MR MR MAIR! This is our 2nd and final call for action to you. We urgently request that you finally give us the order by return, to ship a maximum of 2 FREE PREMIUM PACKAGES + A CHEQUE.' The top prize could be for as much as ten thousand pounds.

Elsewhere, the envelope was busy with FINAL CALL FOR ACTION! On the back, code numbers that could apparently get me a free curved TV, a camcorder and an iPhone. It was very important I scratch the panel on the express stamp immediately or people would die.

Concerned that the breathless offers of endless free money and gadgets would not stop Mr Mr Mair from throwing it all in the recycling, the front of the envelope also boasted 'Enclosed: free hand cream sample. Quick. Try it out.' In the high-energy world of marketing envelopes, even the free hand cream must be tested at once.

By this stage all I wanted to know was who was behind this fantastic piece of work. I was moments away from discovering the exciting product responsible for the most thrilling mail to arrive in months.

My nervous fingers ripped at the envelope. A forest of bright paperwork tumbled out that made the election litera-ture look like a limerick. Where, oh where, in all the garish, hyperventilated leaflets was the product they were selling?

Finally, I found it. It was a gardening catalogue. I cried

with joy until the tears stained my face. And then I wiped the tracks with the hand cream.

28 May–3 June

Full speed ahead

My whirlwind weekend in Istanbul

A quick weekend jaunt to Istanbul. Forty-eight hours to sample the city that used to be called Constantinople – now it's Istanbul, not Constantinople, and that's nobody's business but the Turks'.

The taxi driver from the airport propelled himself to number one in my list of Global Scary Taxi Drivers. He pushed the stoned San Francisco cabbie into second place, and the deranged Hong Kong driver with the knife in his glove compartment into third.

My Turkish friend earned his stars thanks to his foot-to-the-floor treatment of both the accelerator and brake pedals. It was like William Shatner's speech patterns on wheels. I especially enjoyed it when he stopped the car on a tiny triangular chevron on what appeared to be a Grand Prix circuit in order to phone a friend to ask where my hotel was. As cars zoomed past my earlobe I assumed death was imminent and closed my eyes to see what my flashback entailed. It was mainly ill-judged questions and awkward silences. It's been a good life.

I knew I was still alive when I felt the G-force of acceleration as Turkey's Stirling Moss pulled out into the speeding traffic, zipping into any space in any lane that appeared to be car-sized. In fairness to him, everyone else on the road appeared to have gone to the same driving school. Car horns were sounded so liberally I assumed there was a clown convention in town.

Ninety exhilarating minutes later – much of it in stationary traffic that caused my driver enormous irritation – we arrived at the hotel. I paid him, tipped him and gave him some blood-pressure medicine, and we went our separate ways.

Actually, the hotel only let us stop outside after the taxi was checked by security staff for bombs. I'm not joking. The full mirror-under-the-vehicle treatment. My hotel, in common with many others I saw later, had barriers and security staff vetting every entrant. Once in the building, airport-style scanners checked people and luggage. We're all at risk of terrorist attacks just about anywhere but Turkey, as you know, has multiple groups interested in causing death and destruction. I was told that the threat of violence has caused a big drop in tourist numbers: that one big airline recently cancelled many of its daytime flights to Istanbul. The hotel security made me feel good that they took everyone's safety so seriously, and at the same time sad that it was deemed necessary.

A tram to the old town took me to the Grand Bazaar, the wildly popular and enormous indoor market that had cornered the market in markets before London's Westfield was even thought of. Here my backpack was wanded for explosives, and quite right too. A bomb in those crowded historic alleyways would cause unimaginable harm to humans, and devastate the world's supply of knock-off Yves Saint Laurent.

Istanbul has dazzling mosques, the most Bosphorus-y stretch of water you'll find anywhere and a fine, if somewhat complicated, underground system. The population appears to increase by a million a minute, so you're never short of company. I took some pleasure in ferrying to Asian Turkey and stepping away into residential neighbourhoods where people looked down at me from their open windows and thought, what's that bloody tourist doing here?

Oh, and I do recommend the Turkish coffee. Or, as they call it there, coffee.

18–24 June

What about me?

The day I lost out to a baby

In the news business, timing is everything. What else was happening in the world on the day Kennedy was assassinated, or on 9/11, or on the day Peggy Mitchell died? It's hard to say because the news was dominated by those single events.

And so it is in life. Timing is everything, as I was reminded recently when a relative celebrated a birthday.

Thirty years ago, when I was twenty, I was trying to pass my driving test. I had had two or perhaps three unsuccessful attempts. It was becoming a cause of some frustration for me that I was repeatedly unable to navigate the heavily junctioned streets of Broughty Ferry to the satisfaction of my dashboard-slapping examiner.

None of my test failures featured a damaged bollard or injured pedestrian. I don't recall mounting a pavement or smashing through the window of Dolcis. I was just not quite good enough: something which would become a recurring theme in my career, but let's not get into that vale of tears here.

There I was, with the summer of '86 approaching, still struggling to legally master the art of driving a car. Don't get me wrong, it was a tricky time for everyone. People were anxious about the football World Cup, and 'The Chicken Song' by *Spitting Image* was number one.

I resolved that on this third (or fourth) attempt at passing my driving test I would either succeed or give up. I recall vividly getting into the driver's seat and saying to my examiner, 'Good morning. This may not seem relevant now, but I've a funny feeling that next month England will lose 2–1 to Argentina in the World Cup and Argentina will go on to beat West Germany in the final. Now shall we begin?'

In truth, I remember almost nothing about the test itself, apart from the fact I sweated more than a pig that knows it's dinner. How my hands were still able to grip the steering wheel I have no idea. They were sodden just from the torrents of sweat running down from the faucets that were my armpits. I hoped and prayed the examiner had a reliable valet service, because otherwise this vehicle was a write-off.

Pulling the car up for the final time, I tried to answer his verbal questions with no saliva left in my mouth. If history was any guide, this was to be my most brilliant failure yet.

I could hear the examiner saying I'd passed, and the movement of his lips appeared to concur yet I couldn't quite believe it. I thanked him, and offered to shake his hand, but he just covered my dripping fingers with a wet wipe and ran off.

I arrived home to break the news of my triumph to the family. Finally, I had done it! I ran into the kitchen, heart bursting with pride, and everyone beamed at me: 'Great news! Your sister's had a baby boy!'

Over the years I've learnt to forgive young Ross for his terrible timing. Plus, his recent thirtieth birthday means I know without checking my licence how long I've been driving for. Still. Why couldn't he have waited? I wanted to be the lead story that night.

Age concern

A tip for you. Do not ever – and I mean EVER – take on the mantle of being Britain's oldest person. In my experience, it's a death sentence.

6–12 August

Simply unmissable

My late-night miracle – and a mistake

There's only one Andrew Neil, as I believe they still chant on the terraces at St Mirren. So standing in for him recently on BBC1's *This Week* was a daunting task. If you haven't seen it, and even if you have, it's a political talk show that doesn't take itself too seriously. There are oodles of in-jokes, strange Twitter hashtags for guests, wilfully hammy opening credits, and a powerful sense that perhaps most of the audience is drunk. Andrew is at the centre of it all, growling, provoking and teasing. Sometimes his dog growls too.

I always watch it on catch-up, so the lateness of the live broadcast didn't really hit me until, well, I was sitting on the set at two hours past my regular bedtime, waiting for the opening credits to roll. Who has to pretend to be awake at this hour?

It is a lark, though. The opening credits had a *Star Trek* theme in honour of the new film. For reasons that escape me now, I had to be seen in a *Star Trek* T-shirt, swigging from a bottle of gold Blue Nun, while pretending to judder, as you do in space. There's talk of a BAFTA nod, but for me the work is its own reward.

Andrew wasn't far away, even though he was. He popped up in film form from the US, and at the last minute a plan was hatched to have his face appear on the sofa next to me, on a small TV. Just before air-time there was some fiddling to get the TV to stay upright. Andrew's face was on two red cushions and the telly was propped up by a china teapot round the back of the screen. Michael Portillo thought that perhaps Andrew was leaning a bit to the right, but I think it was straight enough on screen.

Before, during and after the show was relaxed and convivial. Warm hellos from the regular guests as they arrived, gossiping in huddles about politics and, in the case of the SNP MP John Nicolson, his splendid home renovations.

Pre-show catering extended to salted peanuts, but afterwards some chocolates and wine to mark the end of the series. I hadn't caused that; it was just the last one before recess. It will be back in the autumn – give it a whirl.

Perhaps I can blame being tired from *This Week* for an especially ghastly mistake on *PM* the following night. Throughout the programme, introducing the news bulletins at 5 and 5.30, and the headlines at 5.15, I intoned that Luke Tuddenham was reading the news. He wasn't. The news was being read – superbly as always – by Howard Philpott.

Here's the classy thing about Howard. Although he would have been entitled to say, on air, 'Ahem, it's not Luke, it's Howard', he didn't: he read the news without saying a word about my rude mistake. It was all my fault. The name Howard Philpott was in the script, but somehow I'd written Luke's name in my usual failsafe way on a piece of paper in front of me, and so introduced Luke every time.

It was only when another Radio 4 announcer, Neil Sleat, messaged me after the 5.30 summary on the internal computer system to gently point out my mistake that I realised.

I'm such a prat. I apologised profusely to Howard, who waved away my protestations. Not sure I would have been so generous. Here's to you Howard: a professional, having to put up with an amateur.

15–21 October

My blue hell

Following in the Smurfs' footsteps

On my recent holiday I took a break from my tireless charity work in Africa and plastic surgery appointments in Switzerland to tootle around Andalusia. People rave about hiking and getting off the beaten track but, for me, it's hard to beat a good tootle.

As you may know, that part of Spain is dotted with pretty villages, all as white as the Academy Awards or a Donald Trump rally. Each has a church every twenty yards and only one shop, which never seems to be open. Some Spanish hamlets (*jamón pequeño?*) are less pretty close up than they seem from a distance, but then so am I.

One day, during a pre-tootle google, I read that there was a most unusual town called Júzcar. Its claim to fame is that five years ago the whole place was painted blue to publicise a film. I'm not sure if you're familiar with the Smurfs' oeuvre – I confess it's on my to-do list – but in 2011 a Smurfs movie came out. It was set in New York, where the little blue creatures got lost. One of the geniuses at the film's marketing department thought it would be a wheeze to paint an entire Andalusian town blue and stage the Smurfs' world premiere there. I'm not making this up.

Everyone in Júzcar went along with this, presumably having also smoked whatever they were taking in the marketing department. Reportedly, the town, which previously attracted three hundred visitors a year, was suddenly welcoming eighty thousand. The deal was that, six months after the premiere, Sony would send in the painters with several million gallons of white paint. But the people of Júzcar were so thrilled with their new-found fame that they opted to stay blue.

I had to see it for myself.

Getting to Júzcar was something of a faff. It's not a million miles from Ronda and all its glories, but it's accessed via an ever-worsening and narrowing set of roads. The scenery en route was stunning, with countless pretty white villages dotting the landscape.

The slightly scary drive came to an end when, up ahead, there was the unmistakably blue town. After parking, I got out into the searing heat and took in the blue view. I haven't seen anything that blue since the night Nick Ferrari of LBC was nominated for five Sony awards and unforgivably didn't get any. Not a wall or doorstep in the town was un-blue. It felt like a parallel universe or an optical illusion. My brain was telling me everything should be white, but every square inch was Smurf-blue.

A restaurant (painted blue) seemed busy enough, but in the town itself only a handful of tourists were meandering. Perhaps the numbers were dropping off, five years on. Some walls were also painted with giant Smurfs in various guises. Statues of Smurfs were placed in open areas. For me, it was a little creepy but maybe they're delightful if you've seen the film. After an hour or so I wanted to strangle them and escape. I felt like Patrick McGoohan in *The Prisoner*, only less snappily dressed.

Good luck to the people of Júzcar. Their town is unique. But my advice is: if some animators knock on your door wanting to paint your house Garfield orange, give it serious thought.

29 October–4 November

Age concern

At nearly fifty-one, what should I do next?

Steve Hewlett's appearances on *PM* recently have caused a lot of interest – as did his article for *Radio Times* the other week. Articulate and candid, Steve's response to the cancer that has become part of his life has been admired by many listeners. Last week on *iPM* we heard from one of them – Marcus, recently diagnosed with colon cancer – who listened to Steve in the car with his three teenage children. No one spoke while Steve spoke, and Marcus told me his family all benefited from Steve's words.

I try not to turn this column into a dreary plug for stuff I do, but given the impact of Steve's broadcasts, can I point you gently towards something called the Eddie Mair Interview Podcast? The title was not my idea, you'll be surprised to learn. Search online for it, or use your favourite podcast app on your phone, tablet or tin foil on your head, and you'll find all Steve's stuff, as well as some other interesting people. If you subscribe (it's free), you'll never miss a thing. I should also alert you to Steve's *Media Show* podcast but frankly he can do his own hustling.

All that talk of diagnoses and prognoses can lead to neuroses. Usually when radio presenters ask 'How long have I got?', it's to establish an interview's duration. Hearing from Steve, Marcus and others throws all our lives into sharper relief.

Last November I turned fifty. Fifty-one is looming in a few days and I've been turning my attention to what to do next in life. Too many people I know have worked feverishly until retirement, only to drop dead within months. Others, around my age, get life-changing news from their doctors – for them the retirement dream is no longer an option. Others still struggle into their eighties and nineties battling poverty, dementia and loneliness.

Depressing, isn't it?

So here is a true story about ageing that happened to me last Saturday.

London seemed especially busy and tiresome, so, over lunch with a chum, we discussed which coastal resorts we could faff about in for the afternoon. Southend-on-Sea was a virgin location for us both, and in short order we were at West Ham station waiting for the train.

Sir John Betjeman once said, 'The Pier is Southend, Southend is the Pier.' In the brief late afternoon we had, Southend was indeed the Pier. Goodness, it's long. From the Western Esplanade it made Brighton Pier look like a mini-roundabout. Off we strode to the entrance.

It was two pounds each to walk the pier, and I eagerly proffered four pound coins to the woman behind the glass. At this point, my friend thought it amusing to pipe up, 'Isn't it only a pound for the over-sixties?', gesturing at me.

'Oh, sorry,' said the woman. She smiled benignly at me, and handed back one pound, along with a receipt showing I had paid for a concession fare. I still have the receipt. My first ever concession fare. It is downhill from here.

It's a mile and a third to the end of the pier and I swear to you my so-called friend laughed the whole way. At fifty, I had been accepted for sixty.

At the end of the pier I generously dropped my saved pound into the swirly RNLI donation box. Southend Pier's loss was the charity's gain, and they do tremendous work. I felt a bit less like a thief.

Then I pushed my friend into the Thames and really got my money's worth.

5–11 November

Time for a change

What happened to the in-depth interview?

This week finally brings the US Presidential election. The campaign has gone on longer than *An Evening with Ken Dodd* but has left few people tickled. It's cost even more than that new Netflix drama about the Queen, but without Peter Morgan's snappy dialogue.

Supporters of that system say it tests the candidates and their policies. I don't doubt that it stretches a politician's stamina. But how much have the policies really been tested?

The TV debates were mesmerising television, but, despite the efforts of the moderators, especially Chris Wallace in the final encounter, sloganising triumphed over policy analysis.

Where could voters turn to find the candidates truly challenged on the details, the contradictions, their own records? A news conference?

Hillary Clinton has been criticised for holding fewer news conferences than the Queen. Donald Trump has held such events, but has routinely banned reporters from news organisations he dislikes. Even when news conferences are held, the format allows politicians to hide behind sound-bites. Hacks get one question each; detailed follow-ups are impossible.

Where were the one-to-one lengthy interviews? For months the airwaves have been full of the candidates' surro-gates and supporters trading barbs. But Clinton and Trump have been kept away from detailed encounters that would allow exploration of their political beliefs. You want to see them smiling and waving into the middle distance? Sure. How about a photo op holding a glass of locally brewed beer? Fine. But could you see an independent journalist grill them on their policies for an hour? No siree.

In this country too, elections have become filled with smiley events, and when polling day has passed the fashion for many political parties is to keep their stars away from close-questioning by hacks. Survive twenty minutes with Andrew Marr or Robin Prestwick on a Sunday morning. Get through sixty minutes of breakfast interviews split between *Today*, 5 Live, BBC *Breakfast*, *Good Morning Britain*, LBC and Sky News, and then go quiet for six months.

I don't blame politicians or their staff for this. Why run a marathon when you can do a hundred metres? Why sit down with someone who knows what they're talking about when you can spit a few words directly to millions of Twitter followers? Perhaps I'm making an analogue argument in a digital age.

Interviewers must also consider their own failings. I for one have asked dumb questions, pursued pointless arguments and generally let down the listener more often than I can remember. I regret sometimes appearing to be more interested in gaffes than the details. Naturally I blame the producers for this.

This is not a plea for me to get work. I write as a voter who wants our fine journalists to be allowed the time and space to make a complicated world clearer through well-briefed, forensic questioning lasting longer than eight minutes.

The proper interview is not a cure for democracy's ills. Journalists are not perfect and there is a danger they could have too much influence. Politicians should also be allowed to do things without having to pop into a studio every five minutes to explain themselves. But our system leaves this voter hungry for information.

10–16 December

Clear as mud

I'm clearly committed to translating MPs

I'm greatly enjoying some new political phraseology. Well, not new exactly, but it's more fashionable, more noticeable, than it was previously. It's right up there with the time-honoured moment politicians chuck the word 'clearly' into a sentence. On rare occasions it's utilised to bolster a statement about the blindingly obvious: 'Clearly, the sky is blue.' But most often the word is innocently dropped into a sentence riddled with uncertainty.

'Clearly, Brexit means Brexit' is a good example. It might be clear to you. It might be clear to me. But for clarity it's not up there with the sky being blue. Yet we're tempted to believe that the person uttering it believes that what follows the word 'clearly' is in fact clear. The true power of these words is sometimes bolstered with the preface 'As I've said before, many times, clearly, Brexit means Brexit.' A reassuring nod to the casual listener that, however vague this sentence might be, the speaker has been a consistent supporter of its vagueness for a long time.

Clearly is a versatile word. Listen out for it in sentences such as: 'Clearly, there is no disunity in the Labour Party'; 'Clearly, there will be a second independence referendum'; 'Clearly, the Liberal Democrats are on their way back'.

My problem is not about the wisdom or otherwise of any of those utterances – just that we shouldn't pretend that the nuanced grey areas of politics are clear. Perhaps they teach the word clearly in some of the more bargain-basement media training courses. You'd hope it would be clear how clearly annoying it is.

Which brings me to my new bugbear: committed.

It's a word that hints at being a promise, but doesn't actually say so. It suggests aspiration without detailing what action will achieve it. It suggests belief and passion but without the nasty side-effect of explaining what policies will render the commitment a success.

It crops up in manifestos. Rising homelessness is terrible and we're 'committed' to reversing it, said one. How? Apparently by tackling the causes of homelessness. Another talked about a new tax the party was 'committed' to introducing. Not as straightforward as saying 'We will introduce this tax', but something that hints at a direction of travel. Then there is the pledge that a party 'remains committed to' something. It means they've never achieved it, but still really want it – just don't press them on the details.

My name is Eddie Mair. Let me make one thing absolutely clear. I am committed to world peace. I have always been committed to a world where no one goes hungry, where disease is eradicated. Where the natural world thrives alongside humanity, and where American elections don't take quite so long. I am also committed to becoming King of Mexico.

Those are my commitments. I have absolutely no idea how to achieve any of them, but with goals like these, how can you not like me? May I have your vote anyway?

To buy any of our books and to find out
more about Abacus and Little, Brown, our authors
and titles, as well as events and book clubs,
visit our website

www.littlebrown.co.uk

and follow us on Twitter

@AbacusBooks
@LittleBrownUK